Harald Kotlarz / Mary Ratcliffe / Petra Lihocky

Klassenarbeiten wie in der Schule Englisch 5. – 8. Klasse

Gymnasium

Die Audio-Dateien für die Aufgaben zum Hörverstehen findest du zum Download unter www.klett.de/lernhilfen.

Gib dazu den Online-Link 927213-000 in das Suchfeld oben links ein.

Klett Lerntraining

Autoren
Klassenarbeiten 5/6: 01 – 12 **Harald Kotlarz/Mary Ratcliffe**
Klassenarbeiten 7/8: 01 – 06 **Harald Kotlarz/Mary Ratcliffe**
07 – 12 **Petra Lihocky**

Bildquellennachweis:
S. 56: Declan Gelbraith, Portrait 2007: Picture Alliance, Soeren Stache, Frankfurt; S. 70: Papageientaucher: Dietrich Schulz, Schwäbisch Gmünd; Shetland Ruine: Corbis, Frans Lemmens, Düsseldorf; Shetland Boot: shutterstock, Ivan Cholakov, New York; S. 93: Jamie Oliver: Ullstein Bild GmbH, Berlin, 2005; S. 101: The Harrogate Band: www.harrogateband.org, 2005; Norfolk broads: INTERFOTO, München, 2008; Great Orme castle: www.greatorme.org/uk/conwy.html, Noel Walley, 2008; Chester walls: www.chester360.co.uk/pics/chester_walls.jpg, Harrison Associates; Mount Snowdon: Robert Harding Picture Library Ltd.

Der Verlag hat sich nach bestem Wissen und Gewissen bemüht, alle Inhaber von Urheberrechten ausfindig zu machen. Sollte das in irgendeinem Fall nicht korrekt geschehen sein, bitten wir um Entschuldigung und werden selbstverständlich in der nachfolgenden Auflage einen korrigierten Quellennachweis anzeigen.

Bibliografische Information der Deutschen Bibliothek
Die Deutsche Bibliothek verzeichnet diese Publikation in der Deutschen Nationalbibliografie; detaillierte bibliografische Daten sind im Internet über http://dnb.ddb.de abrufbar.

Auflage 4. 3. 2. 1. | 2014 2013 2012 2011
Die letzten Zahlen bezeichnen jeweils die Auflage und das Jahr des Druckes.

Internetadresse: www.klett.de/lernhilfen
Covergestaltung: Martin Miersch, Stuttgart
Innengestaltung: Martin Miersch, Stuttgart
Redaktionsassistenz: Verena Malmsheimer
Illustrationen: Marlene Pohle, Stuttgart: S. 15, 16, 18, 19, 21, 28, 29; Lars Benecke, Hannover: S. 43, 48, 78, 84, 116; Michael Luz, Stuttgart: S. 65; Yousun Koh, Münster: S. 137, 138, 152; Katja Rau, Fellbach: S. 152; Helga Merkle, Albershausen: S. 152; Klett-Archiv, Stuttgart: S. 152; Athos Boncompagni, Arezzo – Italy: S. 152.
Satz: DTP-studio Andrea Eckhardt, Göppingen
Druck: Medienhaus Plump, Rheinbreitbach
Printed in Germany
ISBN 978-3-12-927213-8

9 783129 272138

Inhaltsverzeichnis

KLASSENARBEITEN FÜR DIE 7./8. Klasse

LÖSUNGEN Klassenarbeiten 5./6. Klasse

LÖSUNGEN Klassenarbeiten 7./8. Klasse

So hilft dir das Buch!

Liebe Schülerin, lieber Schüler

Du willst **perfekt vorbereitet** in die nächste **Klassenarbeit** gehen?
Dann teste dich mit unseren „Klassenarbeiten" und du wirst wissen, wie gut du bist.

Die **24 Klassenarbeiten** in diesem Buch decken alle **wichtigen Themen** der Klassen 5–8 im Fach Englisch ab.
Jede Klassenarbeit ist auf **45 Minuten** angelegt und allen Aufgaben sind **Punkte** zugeordnet – **wie in der Schule**.

Mit den **ausführlichen Lösungen** kannst du ohne fremde Hilfe kontrollieren, ob du alles richtig gemacht hast. Dann weißt du auch genau, was der Lehrer von dir erwartet.

Zusätzliche Tipps bei den Lösungen geben dir Hinweise auf besondere **Stolpersteine** und erinnern dich an wichtige **Regeln** und **Formeln**.
Deine **Note** kannst du sofort in der Tabelle ablesen, wenn du alle erreichten Punkte zusammengezählt hast.

In den meisten Klassenarbeiten sind Aufgaben zum Hörverstehen enthalten. Du erkennst sie an folgendem Zeichen.
Um sie bearbeiten zu können, benötigst du Audio-Dateien, die wir dir unter folgender Adressse zum Download zur Verfügung stellen:
www.klett.de/lernhilfen.
Auf dieser Seite gibst du oben links den **Online-Link 927213-0000** ein, dann kannst du die Dateien im mp3-Format herunterladen.

So benutzt du das Buch:

45 Minuten

Zeitvorgabe
An jeder Klassenarbeit findest du eine Zeitvorgabe. Nimm dir eine Uhr und versuche innerhalb der angegebenen Zeit die Aufgaben selbstständig zu lösen.

1/6 Blätter

Organisation
Die Blattangabe hilft dir bei der Zeiteinteilung – so siehst du schnell, wie viele Seiten du in der vorgegebenen Zeit noch bearbeiten musst.

Lösung S. 165

Lösungen
An jeder Klassenarbeit steht direkt, wo du die zugehörigen Lösungen findest. Das verschafft dir einen schnellen Überblick und verhindert lästiges Blättern.

Schritt 1
Suche dir im Inhaltsverzeichnis die Klassenarbeit zu den Stoffgebieten heraus, die du gerade in der Schule behandelst.

Schritt 2
Nimm dir die angegebene Zeit und versuche, die Aufgaben selbstständig zu lösen. Lege dir auch alle zusätzlich benötigten Materialien, Stifte, Papier usw. bereit.

Die Hörverstehenstexte werden von Muttersprachlern in authentischem Sprachtempo vorgetragen. Wenn du noch etwas ungeübt bist, kannst du dir das Anhören mithilfe der Pausentaste und durch wiederholte Wiedergabe erleichtern. Zusätzlich sind alle Texte bei den Lösungen abgedruckt. Du kannst sie dort nachlesen.

01
KLASSENARBEIT

45 Minuten

1/7 Blätter

Lösung S. 166

EXERCISE 1

Listening comprehension | Track 1

Listen to the girl and underline the right words or numbers.

Name:	Jane / Gina / Jean
From:	Bromley / Bristol / Brisbane
Age:	10 / 11 / 12
New in Bromley:	Yes / No
New friends:	Rachel and Thomas / Steven and Rachel / Steven and Lisa
Favourite sport:	tennis / football / volleyball

__ / 6 P.

EXERCISE 2

Reading comprehension

Schritt 3
Vergleiche dein Ergebnis mit der Musterlösung hinten im Buch und korrigiere dich.

LÖSUNG ZU AUFGABE 3

Mediation

Übersetze die Sätze und schreibe sie auf.

a) Write in your exercise books, please.
b) Thank you.
c) Now there is one crisp.
d) There's a mouse in my bag.

Gib dir für jeden richtigen Satz 1 Punkt.

Schritt 4
Gib dir jetzt Punkte. Die Gesamtpunktzahl, die du erreichen kannst, steht neben der Aufgabe. Die genaue Aufteilung der Punkte – welche Leistung wie viele Punkte ergibt – siehst du in den Lösungen in der rechten Seitenspalte.

GESAMT
___ / 65 P.

Schritt 5
Zähle deine Punkte zusammen und lies in der Tabelle ab, welche Note du erreicht hast.

MEIN ERGEBNIS

Punkte	61–57	56–54	53–49	48–46	45–40	39–37	36–31	30–28	27–17	16	15–0
Note	1	1,5	2	2,5	3	3,5	4	4,5	5	5,5	6

5. / 6. Klasse

01 KLASSENARBEIT

45 Minuten

1/7 Blätter

Lösung S. 166

EXERCISE 1

Listening comprehension | Track 1

Listen to the girl and underline the right words or numbers.

Name:	Jane / Gina / Jean
From:	Bromley / Bristol / Brisbane
Age:	10 / 11 / 12
New in Bromley:	Yes / No
New friends:	Rachel and Thomas / Steven and Rachel / Steven and Lisa
Favourite sport:	tennis / football / volleyball

_/6 P.

EXERCISE 2

Reading comprehension

a) Read the text.

It's English now with Mr Watson.

Mr Watson:	Now do the exercise on page twelve. Write in your exercise books, please.
David:	Sorry, Mr Watson, but where is the exercise?
Mr Watson:	Listen, please, David. It's on page twelve.
David:	Okay. Thank you.
Steven:	This exercise is easy.
David:	No, it isn't. Look. "Fill in the right words". That isn't easy.
Steven:	Look, David! There's a mouse. A tiny mouse. Now it's behind the door. Oh, there are two crisps behind the door. Now there is one crisp … and now there isn't a crisp there.
David:	It's a nice mouse.
Mr Watson:	What's the problem now, David?
David:	Oh, no problem, Mr Watson. But the exercise isn't easy.
Mr Watson:	Start the exercise, David. Find the right words and put them in.
Steven:	Watch out, David. The mouse is in your bag. Where are your sandwiches?

David: In my bag, of course. Oh …

Mr Watson: David! Do the exercise. Copy the text and write the answers!

David: There's a mouse in my bag.

Mr Watson: Very funny. Now do the exercise.

b) Put a cross by the right picture.

a) Here is the teacher:

○ **A**

☒ **B**

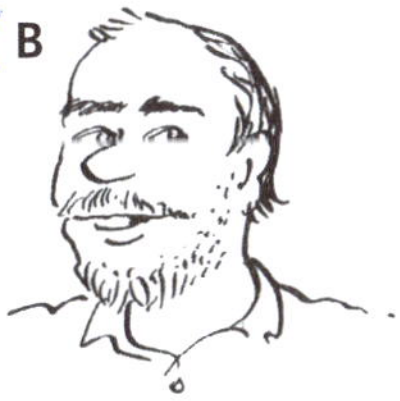

○ **C**

b) This is the right page:

☒ **A**

○ **B**

○ **C**

c) The exercise looks like this:

○ **A:** 5193 + 187 + 2916

☒ **B:** 'Write a story about a mouse'

☒ **C:** __ boys are ____ the playground and the ball ____ in a tree.

c) Here are the crisps:

☒ A

○ B

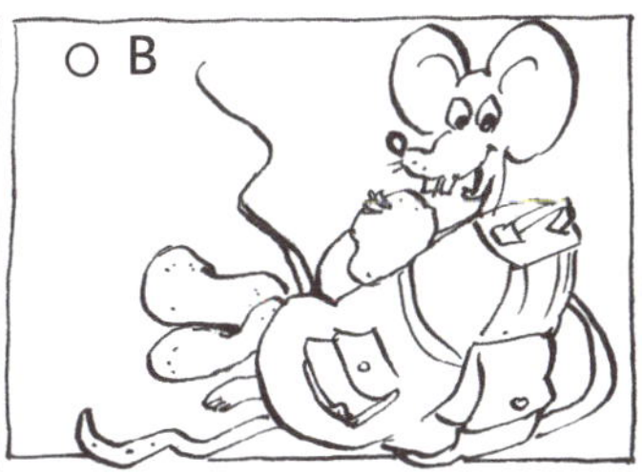

○ C

d) Here is David's bag:

e) This is Mr Watson:

☒ A

○ B

○ C

__/6 P.

EXERCISE 3

Mediation

Find the English in the text and write it.

a) Schreibt bitte in eure Hefte. Write in your exercise books, please.

b) Danke. Thank you

c) Jetzt gibt es einen Kartoffelchip. Now there is one crisp.

d) In meiner Tasche ist eine Maus. There's a mouse in my bag

__/4 P.

EXERCISE 4

Writing

Name: David Thornton (Age 11)

New in Bromley? No

Favourite sport: football

Friends: Steven, Paul, Rachel

You are David. Write a text. Start like this:

My name is David Thornton. I'm not new in Bromley. My favourite sport is football. Steven, Paul and Rachel are my friends.

___/9 P.

EXERCISE 5

Put the word or words in the right box.

apple • unit • folder • bag • answer • big apple • classroom • old car • English book • exercise book

a	an
unit	apple
folder	answer
bag	old car
big apples	an English book
a classroom	an exercise book

___/5 P.

EXERCISE 6

Where are the things?

on • in • under • in front of • behind

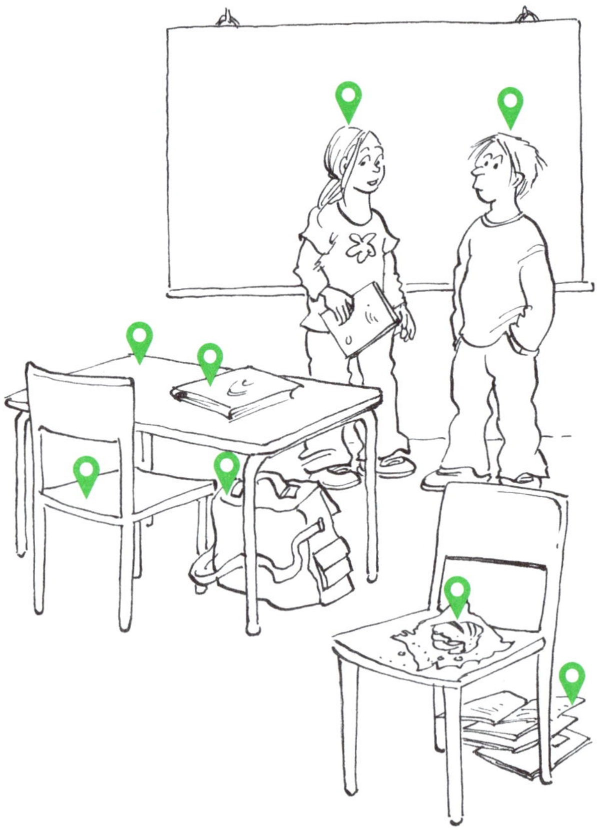

a) *The book is* ______________________________

b) *The schoolbag is* ______________________________

c) *The exercise books are* ______________________________

d) ______________________________

e) ______________________________

f) ______________________________

__ / 6 P.

EXERCISE 7

Complete the sentences. In Rachel's classroom there are ...

Example: *In Rachel's classroom there are 28 pupils.*

a) 30  *There are* ______________________________

b) 4  ______________________________

c) 15  ______________________________

d) 28  ______________________________

e) 2  ______________________________

f) 1  ______________________________

__/6 P.

EXERCISE 8

Ask the questions. Use: *where – who – what.*

Example: She's in the classroom. → *Where is Sarah?*

a) They are in the playground. ______________________________

b) It's our new teacher. ______________________________

c) She's from Germany. ______________________________

d) Her name is Mrs Schneider. ______________________________

e) I'm her friend. ______________________________

__/10 P.

EXERCISE 9

Put in a good adjective.

big • old • cool • boring • nice • new • wrong • useful

a) Football is a ______________________________ sport.

b) I'm sorry, but this answer is ______________________________.

c) Is your schoolbag ______________________________?

d) My school is so ______________________________.

e) Your jokes aren't funny, they're ______________________________.

__ / 5 P.

EXERCISE 10

Find the people and write them out.

chairfriendteacherschoolcrispbagfavouriteexercisetutorpupilfunnycaretakergamegirlthisboyshoemum

____

____

__ / 4 P.

GESAMT

___ / 61 P.

02
KLASSENARBEIT

45 Minuten

1/4 Blätter

Lösung S. 169

EXERCISE 1

Listening comprehension | Track 2

a) Anne is at Rachel's house. Tick the right picture.

A ☐

B ☐

C ☐

b) Now Rachel's dad is here. Which picture is right?

A ☐

B ☐

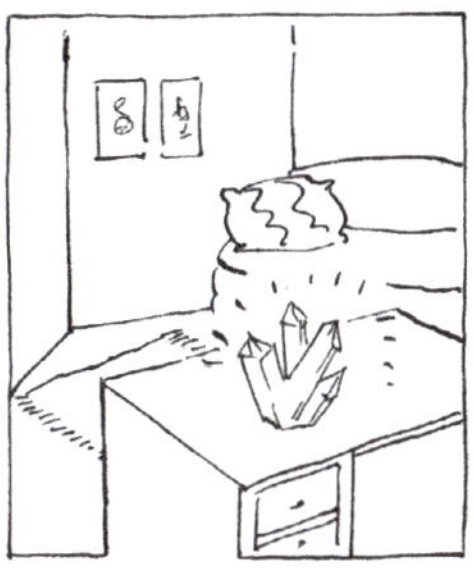

C ☐

__/4 P.

EXERCISE 2

Reading comprehension

Hello Barbara,
My name is Rachel Hill and I'm eleven. I've got a big sister, Liz. She's thirteen. And I've got a little brother, Jack. **(A)** He's a pain, but he's sweet, too. My mum's name is Linda. She's English. My dad's name is Tony. He's half English and half Polish, because his mother is Polish. So I've got a Polish grandmother, but she isn't in Poland. **(B)** Her name is Rose. We've got a house with a small garden. There's a shed in the garden. Liz and I have got our bikes in the shed. Jack hasn't got a bike. I've got my own room. It's very small, so I haven't got a wardrobe or a desk in my room. Liz has got a big wardrobe for her things and my things. And I've got a desk in her room. There are always problems with her room, so we've got rules about it. But they're her rules, not my rules, and that's a problem, too! I've got a laptop in my room, because a laptop is only small. My laptop is with my books. Have you got a sister or a brother? How old are they and what are their names? **(C)**
Write soon, please.
Love, Rachel

a) Put a cross by the right answer.

1. How old is Rachel's sister?
   ○ 13 ○ 14 ○ 15
2. What is Rachel's grandmother's name?
   ○ Rose ○ Linda ○ Liz
3. Where is Rachel's bike?
   ○ in the house ○ in the shed ○ in the garden
4. What has Rachel got in her room?
   ○ a wardrobe and a laptop ○ only a wardrobe
   ○ only a laptop

b) Three sentences are missing in the reading text. They are here. Put the letters A, B, C in the right places.

______ Have you got your own room?

______ He's four years old.

______ She's here in London.

_ / 7 P.

EXERCISE 3

This is Rachel's family and flat. Put in:

my • your • his • her • our • their.

Anne: There's a chemistry set on the desk. Is it ____________ chemistry set?

Rachel: Yes, it is. And this is ____________ new bed. My old bed is for Jack. It's in ____________ room now.

Anne: Has your sister got ____________ own room?

Rachel: Yes, she has. But we can do ____________ homework in the living room.

Anne: Your mum and dad are nice. Is that ____________ bedroom?

Rachel: No, it isn't. It's Jack's room. Just look at ____________ room. What a mess!

__/7 P.

EXERCISE 4

Make sentences about Rachel Hill's family and their flat.

Example: Tony – Rachel – father → *Tony is Rachel's father.*

a) Liz – Rachel – sister

____

b) The Hills – flat – in Croydon Road

____

c) The girls – wardrobe – problem

____

d) Jack – Rachel – little brother

____

e) Her parents – bedroom – big

____

__/10 P.

EXERCISE 5

Have you got an elephant in your room?

Ask questions and give short answers: ☺ = Yes, … ☹ = No, …

Example: elephant in your room ☺

→ *Have you got an elephant in your room? – Yes, I have.*

a) you … desk in your room ☺

____

b) you … two bedrooms ☹

____

c) your brother … own computer ☹

____

d) your parents … two cars ☺

____

What have you got or what haven't you got in your room?
Write two sentences.

e) ____

f) ____ __ / 12 P.

EXERCISE 6

Write four rules for Liz's and Rachel's rooms. Use the reading text (Ex. 2) for ideas.

Example: *Don't use your sister's MP3 player.* __ / 8 P.

GESAMT

___ / 48 P.

03

KLASSENARBEIT

45 Minuten

1 / 4 Blätter

Lösung S. 171

EXERCISE 1

Listening comprehension | Track 3

Mr Large has got a list of clubs at Bromley School. Listen to Mr Large and help Steven with the missing information. Under 'Time' write numbers: 3.30 pm, not: half past three.

Name: *Steven Hall* **Tutor group:** *7UW*

Club	Room	Day of the week	Time	Teacher
Orchestra	________ room	________	3.30 pm – ________	___ White
________ club	Room ________	Tuesday	________ – 5.15 pm	Mr Watson
Internet ________	________ room	Wednesday	________ – 4.45 pm	Mrs Holding
Cooking club	School ________	________	3.15 pm – ________	___ Appleton

__/14 P.

EXERCISE 2

Reading comprehension

Here is a list of the clubs at Bromley School. Find the right club for each child.

Chemistry club	Dancing club	Garden club	Orchestra
Cooking club	Film club	Internet café	Pet club

Andy is interested in music. He plays the drums. His drum lesson is every Wednesday at half past four. He has got drums in his bedroom at home. The neighbours aren't always happy about that!

Club: ________________________________

Steven loves his dog. He walks the dog every weekend and he feeds the dog every day. He likes cats, too, but dogs and cats aren't usually friends, so he hasn't got a cat. He sometimes feeds his friend's mice.

Club: ________________________________

Anne helps her mum in the kitchen at the weekends. She reads books about food. She can make a good chocolate cake. Sometimes she makes lunch for the family. Then her mum can read a book or go shopping. When she gets home, the lunch is on the table.

Club: ______________________________

Josie likes role play at school, and she goes to the cinema with her dad every Saturday. After the film, they talk about it.

Club: ______________________________

Paul hasn't got a computer at home. But he says computers are great. He likes computer games, and he sometimes plays with his neighbour's computer. They find information together. Sometimes that helps with Paul's homework.

Club: ______________________________

__ / 5 P.

EXERCISE 3

Put a cross in the right place.

a) **Andy:**
I ○ play ○ the ○ drums ○ after ○ school. *usually*

b) **Steven:**
My brother ○ and I ○ walk ○ the ○ dog on ○ Mondays. *never*

c) **Anne:**
I ○ help ○ mum ○ in ○ the ○ kitchen ○ at weekends. *often*

d) **Josie:**
I ○ go ○ to ○ the ○ cinema ○ with ○ my dad. *always*

e) **Paul:**
We ○ can ○ play ○ computer games ○ at my home. *sometimes*

f) **Anne:**
It's ○ fun ○ to make ○ lunch ○ for the family. *always*

__ / 6 P.

EXERCISE 4

Find the right verb. Do not forget the third person singular *-s*.

be • like • get up • play • live • go

Andy ____________ the drums every day. Mr Spencer ____________ in the house next to him. And he ____________ not happy about it. Mr Spencer ____________ music, but not drums in the evening. He usually ____________ at 5.30 am and so he ____________ to bed early.

_/6 P.

EXERCISE 5

Say it again.

Example: Anne: I never go to school on Sundays.

→ *She never goes to school on Sundays.*

a) **Josie:** I often talk about films. ______________________________

b) **Anne:** I never cook on Fridays. ______________________________

c) **Paul:** I play computer games at my neighbour's house. ____________

d) **Mr Watson:** I watch a lot of films. ____________________________

e) **Mr Appleton:** I make cakes with the pupils. ____________________

f) **Steve:** I like to walk the dog. ______________________________

_/6 P.

EXERCISE 6

Put in the missing letters.

a) everyw____ere b) hom____work c) int____rested

d) import____nt e) cin____ma f) us____ally

_/6 P.

EXERCISE 7

Writing

Look at the pictures. Mr Watson says:
"*Write about your Tuesday afternoon.* Use these words:

first • then • after that • finally

You are Andy. Look at the pictures and write his text."

I usually get home at quarter to four. ______________________

____

______________________ __/8 P.

EXERCISE 8

Fill in the missing word.

Example: grandfather – grandmother / uncle – *aunt*

a) living room – sofa / bedroom – ______________________

b) English – England / German – ______________________

c) bag – exercise book / pencil case – ______________________

d) cupboard – books / wardrobe – ______________________

e) write – story / draw – ______________________ __/5 P.

GESAMT
___/56 P.

04
KLASSENARBEIT

45 Minuten

1/4 Blätter

Lösung S. 174

EXERCISE 1

Listening comprehension | Track 4

Look at the map. Put A, B and C in the right boxes. There are four boxes. Use only three.

A information centre   B swimming pool   C museum

_/6 P.

EXERCISE 2

Reading comprehension

Mr Watson's tutor group read a text every week.
Here is the text for this week.

<u>Bristol</u>
Bristol is a big town in the west of England, near the sea.
It is not very near London. It is about two hours away by car or train.
Bristol has got a museum, a swimming pool and a small zoo. **(A)** But it has got some special sights, too. There is an old ship at Bristol. Its name is the Great Britain, and it is a museum ship. You can go round it and see the tiny bedrooms. **(B)** And you can see the big ship's wheel.
There is a famous bridge in Bristol, too. It is Clifton Suspension Bridge. **(C)**
Bristol has not got an underground and it has not got trams. But it has got buses, of course, and there are a lot of taxis. The taxi drivers are usually nice. **(D)**
There is a big park, too: the Downs. People often park their cars on the road there and walk their dogs on the Downs. The park is in the west of the town, near the zoo.
From Bristol you can have a day out by the sea in Weston-super-Mare. **(E)**
A lot of tourists go there by train.
Or you can go to the Cotswolds, a beautiful, quiet part of England just north of Bristol.
So you see, you can have a great time in and near Bristol.

a) **These five sentences are missing from the text. Read the text and find the right place – A, B, C, D or E – for the sentences. Write the letter by the sentence.**

a) _______ It is only half an hour away by car or train.

b) _______ They can tell you about the sights of Bristol.

c) _______ They're just cupboards for people!

d) _______ You can find those things in every big town.

e) _______ You can use it to go over the River Avon by car or on foot.

b) **Put a cross for *right* or *wrong* for each sentence.**

	right	wrong
a) Bristol has got an old ship, a famous bridge, a park and an underground.	○	○
b) Places near Bristol are London, Weston-super-Mare and the Cotswolds.	○	○
c) Bristol has got a big park near the zoo. People walk their dogs there.	○	○
d) Bristol is a very small town in the west of England.	○	○
e) Two important sights in Bristol are an old ship and a bridge over a river.	○	○

_/10 P.

EXERCISE 3

Answer these questions in whole sentences (c, e, f) or short answers (a, b, d).

a) Has Bristol got a zoo? _______________

b) Does Clifton Suspension Bridge go over the River Severn? _______________

c) Where do many people walk their dogs in Bristol? _______________

d) Are there many taxis in Bristol? _______________

e) What's the name of the old ship in Bristol? _______________

f) How can you get from Bristol to Weston-super-Mare? _______________

_/9 P.

EXERCISE 4

Compare Rachel and Anne.

	Rachel:	Anne:
like football	+	–
play handball	–	–
like parks	+	+
read books	–	+
speak German	–	+
like rap music	+	–

Example: Rachel likes football. Anne doesn't like football.

Rachel and Anne ______

______

______

______

_/10 P.

EXERCISE 5

Write the questions to the anwers.

a) Do you ______
– No, I don't know much about Exeter.

b) ______
– Yes, Exeter has got a beautiful old church.

c) ______
– No, Liz doesn't like old churches.

d) ______
– Yes, I know how to get to Exeter.

e) ______
– The train to Bristol goes at 2.15 pm.

f) ______
– You can take a bus at the station. There are lots of buses for the town centre.

_/9 P.

EXERCISE 6

Think of the town where you live, or a town near your home, and answer the questions with *yes* or *no*.

a) Is it a small town? ____________

b) Has it got a zoo? ____________

c) Has it got a big park? ____________

d) Is there a swimming pool? ____________

e) Is the town in the north of Germany? ____________

f) Has it got an underground? ____________

g) Do a lot of tourists visit the town? ____________

Now use the questions and answers to write a short text about the town.

Start like this: *... is a small / big / nice town. It has got ...*

_ / 12 P.

EXERCISE 7

The German word 'kein' in English. Translate the missing parts.

a) Anne mag keine Katzen. Anne ________________ cats.

b) Mr Hill kann kein Deutsch. Mr Hill ________________ German.

c) Das ist kein Wasser, es ist Limonade. This ____________, it's lemonade.

d) Ich habe keinen eigenen Computer. I ________________ computer.

e) Keine Ahnung. ________________ idea.

_ / 9 P.

GESAMT

___ / 65 P.

05

KLASSENARBEIT

45 Minuten

1/5 Blätter

Lösung S. 177

EXERCISE 1

Listening comprehension | Track 5

Listen to the assistant and the customer. The assistant has got a form. Fill in the right information.

a) What is the customer looking for? ____________________

b) Is it a present? ____________________

c) What size? ____________________

d) How much (money)? under £ ____________________

e) Best colour? ____________________

f) Family name ____________________

g) Phone number ____________________

_/7 P.

EXERCISE 2

Reading comprehension

Read the letter.

Dear Aunt Helen,

How are you? I'm fine. It's my birthday in two weeks, on 15th June. That's Wednesday and I've got school all day, so Mum says I can have my party on the Saturday after my birthday. That's 18th June. Would you like to come? Please bring Philip, too. It's terrible – he's my cousin, but I never see him. Well, not very often.
Why are clothes so expensive? The department store near us has got cool black T-shirts with a picture of my favourite band, the Coconuts. But the T-shirts are £20, and that's too much for me. I would like to buy their new CD, "Rock On", too. It's great. My friend David has got it and we sometimes listen to it together.
I hope you and Philip can come to my party. It isn't at our house. It's at the swimming pool in Wellington Road, so don't forget to bring things for swimming. We want to meet there at 3.30 pm. We can eat at the swimming pool, and then at 6.30 it's time to go home.
I would like to be there until 7.30 pm, but Mum and Dad say 'No!'.
Please write or phone soon and say you can come!

Lots of love, Sarah

a) Aunt Helen wants to put all the important information together. Fill in the information.

Birthday party:

a) Who? ____________________

b) Day of the week ____________________

c) Date ____________________

d) When does it start? ____________________

e) When does it finish? ____________________

f) Where? ____________________

_/6 P.

b) Aunt Helen can come to the party with Philip. She wants to take a nice present.
What would Sarah like? There are two ideas in her letter.

a) ____________________

b) ____________________

_/2 P.

c) Complete the dialogue.

Sarah: Can you come to my birthday party? You've got an invitation.

David: Yes, I can come. When is your birthday? Is it on the same day?

Sarah: My birthday is on ____________________

But the party is the big day for me. Lots of people want to come. I've got a letter from Aunt Helen and Philip. They want to come.

David: Hey, who is this Philip?

Sarah: He's ____________________

David: Oh, I see. The party is at the swimming pool, right? Where do you want to meet? At your house?

Sarah: We can meet ____________________

_/3 P.

EXERCISE 3

Write the date.

Example: the twenty-forth of December → *24th December*

a) the twenty-fifth of April ______________________

b) the second of May ______________________

c) the eighteenth of March ______________________

d) the thirty-first of August ______________________

e) the twenty-third of January ______________________

f) the eleventh of September ______________________

__/6 P.

EXERCISE 4

Ask what these people are doing.

Example: Sarah – write a letter – to Aunt Helen
→ *Is Sarah writing a letter to Aunt Helen?*

a) Aunt Helen – look for – a birthday present – for Sarah?

____

b) David and Philip – make a cake – for Sarah's birthday?

____

c) Sarah – buy – new clothes?

____

d) Sarah's friends – sing a song – for her?

____

e) Sarah – have fun – at her birthday party?

____

f) you – help Sarah – with the food and drinks?

____

__/9 P.

EXERCISE 5

Write what they are not doing. Look at the example.

Example: Aunt Helen – ~~make a cake~~ – ~~for Sarah~~
→ *Aunt Helen isn't making a cake for Sarah.*

a) David – ~~work in the kitchen~~

____

b) Sarah and Aunt Helen – ~~buy~~ – ~~CDs~~

____

c) Philip – ~~write a letter~~ – ~~to Sarah~~

____

d) Philip and David – ~~look for~~ – ~~a T-shirt for Sarah~~

____

e) the children – ~~listen to~~ – ~~CDs~~

____

f) Sarah's mother – ~~have fun~~ – ~~in the kitchen~~

____

_ / 9 P.

EXERCISE 6

Sort the words.

~~money~~ • ~~CDs~~ • time • flour • chocolate • magazines • clothes • milk • packets of crisps • good ideas

We haven't got much …	⟷	We haven't got many …
money		*CDs*

_ / 4 P.

EXERCISE 7

Sarah's friend Olivia / Oliver has got an invitation to the party, too, but she / he can't come. Write her / his e-mail.

Du bist Olivia / Oliver. Sag, dass du jeden Samstag Basketball spielst und deswegen nicht zur Party kommen kannst. Entschuldige dich dafür. Schlag vor, dass ihr euch am Sonntag trefft.
Dann kannst du Sarah ihr Geschenk geben.

____

____

____

____

__/10 P.

EXERCISE 8

Fill in the right prepositions. There is one extra word in the box. You don't need it.

at • for • from • in • of • on • to • under

David's birthday is ____________ July. His party is ____________

Saturday 14th July.

It starts ____________ 4.30 pm. That's when his dad gets home

____________ work. His friends can come ____________ his house.

Then they can go to the swimming pool.

It's not very expensive for children ____________ fourteen years old.

And they can have lots ____________ fun!

__/7 P.

GESAMT

__/ 63 P.

06
KLASSENARBEIT

45 Minuten

1/5 Blätter

Lösung S. 180

EXERCISE 1

Listening comprehension | Track 6

Listen to Rachel. She's phoning Anne. Put Anne's side of the call into the right order.

_____ **Anne:** What is she doing at the moment?

_____ **Anne:** Maybe you can go shopping.

__1__ **Anne:** Oh, hi! Where are you?

_____ **Anne:** Yes, you have. You've got one friend there. Steven is visiting people in Bristol at the moment.

_____ **Anne:** Why? What are they doing?

_____ **Anne:** Oh, men don't usually like shops. What's your dad doing now?

_____ **Anne:** Yes, I have. Have you got a pen? It's 0177-239 5714.

_/7 P.

EXERCISE 2

Reading comprehension

Read the text about Weston-super-Mare.

Most people just call the town 'Weston', but its full name is Weston-super-Mare. The name Weston comes from the words 'west' and 'town'.
The words 'super mare' are Latin and they mean 'on the sea'.

You can get to Weston in a car or on the train. There is a fast train service to Weston from Paddington Station in London.
Buses from the bus company 'First Group' run to towns near Weston.

Weston is in on the Bristol Channel in North Somerset, 18 miles or 28 kilometres south-west of Bristol. 71,758 people live there. This number comes from a count in the year 2001.
Weston's partner town is Hildesheim in Germany.

Weston has got a long, sandy beach, but the sea goes a long way out at low tide *(Ebbe)*, so you often can't see it. It can be over a mile (1.5 kilometres) away.

The water is brown, but it is safe to swim in it. Don't try to walk to the sea at low water. This is not safe, because you can sink into the sand.
You can park your car on the beach in places, but don't drive too near the sea. Cars sink into the sand and they can't get out again.

You can go on the Grand Pier, visit the aquarium or look at the Winter Gardens. Every summer there is a concert, 'T4 on the beach'.
The concert is on television. There is a helicopter show at the end of July, and a motocross race on the beach in October. About 1,400 people are in the race and about 80,000 people watch it.

a) **These questions are missing headings. Put them into the right boxes. There is one extra heading. You don't need it.**

- How can you get to Weston?
- Which towns are near Weston?
- What is the beach like?
- What can tourists do in the town?
- What does the name mean?
- What must tourists know about the beach?
- Where is Weston?

_/6 P.

b) **Find these numbers in the text and mark them with the right letter. Three of the numbers are not in the text!**

A eighty thousand
B seventy thousand, seven hundred and eighty-five
C two thousand and one
D eighty
E one thousand four hundred
F twenty-eight
G eight thousand
H seventy-one thousand, seven hundred and fifty-eight

_/5 P.

EXERCISE 3

Write what usually or often happens and what is happening today or at the moment.

a) Lots of people usually ______________________ (watch) the motorcross race.
Today about 80,000 people ______________________ (watch) the race.

b) The fast train to Weston ______________________ (run) late today.
The trains to Weston ______________________ (not / usually / run) late.

c) Rachel usually ______________________ (build) sand castles when she is at the seaside.
But now she ______________________ (text) her friend Steven.

d) Rachel often ______________________ (writes) postcards from Weston.
At the moment she ______________________ (buy) a few.

e) Her dad usually ______________________ (read) the newspaper on the beach.
But today he ______________________ (not read) the newspaper.

f) At the moment Rachel ______________________ (phone) her friend Anne.
She often ______________________ (phone) her when she's on holiday.

__/12 P.

EXERCISE 4

Find the right word and put in the right form. Here are some verbs you can use. You don't need them all.

text • eat • go • watch • drive • read • ride • do

The Hills often ________________ on holiday to Weston-super-Mare.

But this year they ________________ to Torquay. Usually Mr Hill

________________ the car and his wife ________________

some brochures about the place they want to visit. But today Mrs Hill

________________ and Mr Hill ________________ at the map.

And what ________________ Rachel ________________ ?

Of course, she ________________ Steven.

She never ________________ away without (*ohne*) her mobile phone.

__/9 P.

EXERCISE 5

Fill in *some* or *any*.

Rachel is looking for a souvenir for Anne. Her dad is with her.

Mr Hill: Let's go to that shop. I think they've got __________ great souvenirs.

Rachel: Are you sure? I can't see __________ nice things in the window. Just __________ postcards, but there aren't __________ clothes or bags.

Mr. Hill: You're right. But I can see __________ books over there.

Rachel: Books are very expensive. What about magazines?

(to assistant) Have you got __________ magazines?

Assistant: I'm afraid we haven't got ____________ . But we've got ____________ interesting books of adventures at sea.

Rachel: But these are very expensive and I can't see ____________ cheap books.

Mr Hill: Okay, I can give you ____________ money for a book of seaside stories.

Rachel: Thanks Dad! I like to go shopping with you.

_ / 5 P.

EXERCISE 6

Rachel is texting Steven. Here is her message. Write it out in good English.

hi, anne ses u r in bristol. y r u ther? wat r u doin at the momt? cn we meet on Sat?
im on the beach in weston but i cnt c the sea. hope to c u sn. b gd!
rachel xxx

_ / 10 P.

EXERCISE 7

This is Steven's diary for the weekend. It's Friday now. Write Steven's answer to Rachel in good English. Answer the questions in Rachel's text message.

Friday	*look for a present for Grandad*
Saturday	*Grandad's 70th birthday party*
Sunday	*meet Rachel 11.15 bus station (362 bus from Weston)* *Go to the cinema? (Mr Bean is on)*

_ / 12 P.

GESAMT

___ / 66 P.

07

KLASSENARBEIT

45 Minuten

1/5 Blätter

Lösung S. 183

EXERCISE 1

Listening comprehension | Track 7

Some pupils in 8UW are talking about what they did in the summer holidays. Listen to them, and write the letters A to E by each picture. One picture hasn't got a letter.

1. ☐

2. ☐

3. ☐

4. ☐

5. ☐

6. ☐

_/6 P.

EXERCISE 2

Reading Comprehension

Here is Anne's text about her summer holidays.

In the summer holidays we went to Germany. We arrived in Munich at lunchtime. ... (A) ... She and Uncle Alfred and their children live in Passau, and we stayed with them. Passau has got three rivers, and you can go on boat trips. ... (B) ... We walked up a big hill and saw a castle, too.

> The food in Germany is funny, but it isn't bad. Auntie Jane gave my mum some recipes. ... (C) ... Auntie Jane speaks German, of course, but my mum doesn't speak it. I looked at them yesterday. I learn German at school, but I didn't understand all the words in the recipes.
> One afternoon when we were in Passau, my parents, my aunt and my uncle went out together. ... (D) ... They are nice, but they aren't quiet! They don't speak much English.
> I tried to speak German to them, but they just laughed.

Now I'm back at school, I want to learn lots of German. ... (E) ... At the moment I can't talk to my cousins, and I don't understand the recipe for my aunt's fantastic chocolate cake!

a) **Underline the present tenses <u>in the box</u> in green, and the past tenses in orange.**
Don't use the missing sentences from b).

__/7 P.

b) **These sentences are missing from the text. Put the right letter by each sentence.**

___ I looked after my little cousins.

___ Maybe my aunt and uncle can help me.

___ My aunt picked us up and took us to Passau.

___ They're in German.

___ We went on four different boat trips.

__/5 P.

EXERCISE 3

Write what these pupils did in their summer holidays.

Example: Greg: visit / cousin in Germany
→ *Greg visited his cousin in Germany.*

a) Josh: watch / movies every day ______________________

b) Steve: stay / at home ______________________

c) Christine: climb / mountains in Scotland ______________________

d) Martin: cook / nice dinners for / friends and family ______________________

e) Janice: play / lots of computer games ______________________

f) Susan: help / parents in / shop and earn *(verdienen)* some money

____

_ / 6 P.

EXERCISE 4

Fill in the right simple past form of be. Two of them are negative.

a) The holidays ______________ boring.

b) I ______________ on a farm with my parents for two weeks.

c) There ______________ some nice animals.

d) But there ______________ any young people there.

e) The village ______________ much too quiet.

f) It ______________ my favourite place.

_ / 6 P.

EXERCISE 5

Put the simple past form of the following words into the right box.

have • play • wear • write • jump •
go • finish • get • want • arrive

regular forms	irregular forms
______________	______________
______________	______________
______________	______________

__/5 P.

EXERCISE 6

In the summer holidays, Tanya wrote this postcard to her grandma. Now she is back at school, and the children are writing about their holidays. Write Tanya's report.

Dear Grandma,
We are in Padstow. It's nice. There are lots of boats. We go on boat trips but we don't go swimming, because the water is too cold.
I wear my new sunglasses all the time.
I take the dog out every evening. He meets his new dog-friends, and I buy an ice cream at the café.
I want to meet new friends, too, but it isn't easy.

Love, Tanya

In the summer holidays we went to Padstow. Padstow was nice.

____

____

____

____

__/10 P.

EXERCISE 7

Make a verb in the simple past from the word in bold print.

Example: Steven is a very fast **eater**. Yesterday he __ate__ his lunch in five minutes.

a) Mr Appleton is a **teacher** at Nelson School. He's sixty years old, and he ________________ Rachel's mum when she was a pupil at the school.

b) David is a good football **player**. Last week his team ________________ an important game.

c) The **winners** got a prize. David wasn't very happy, because the other team ________________.

d) Anne's uncle is a **painter**. Last summer he ________________ a picture of Anne.

e) Children in England say '**finders**, keepers' when they find something. Last week Paul ________________ a five-pound note. But he didn't keep it.

__ / 5 P.

GESAMT

___ / 50 P.

08
KLASSENARBEIT

45 Minuten

1/6 Blätter

Lösung S. 186

EXERCISE 1

Listening comprehension | Track 8

Listen to the report about a place on one of the posters.

a) **Which place is the man talking about? Put a cross by the right poster.**

A

B

C

_/2 P.

b) **Fill in the missing words and numbers.**

Write times like this: 8 am/7 pm
Write prices like this: £14.50
Write dates like this: 21st, 4th …

Open every day from ___________ to ___________.

London Pass: free

Adult: £ ___________

Child: £ ___________

Address: County Hall, Westminster ______________ Road

Telephone number: ___________, ___________, 8000

Closes at 3 pm on ________ December, ________ December and ________ December. Closed all day on ________ December.

_/9 P.

EXERCISE 2

Reading comprehension

Last summer, Steven's friend Craig spent a week in London with him. One day, when they were looking for some ideas for a day out, Steven found this information on the Internet.

London Wetlands Centre
The London Wetlands Centre opened in the spring of 2000. A lot of British birds and other small wild animals live in or near water, and here at the Wetlands Centre you can get near to them and watch them. We have 3.4 kilometres of pathways[1] and bridges over lakes[2] and marshes[3]. At the Visitors' Centre there are computers where you can find out more about the animals here. There are cameras at some places in the wetlands, so you can also watch animals and birds from the Visitors' Centre. Tickets cost £8.75 for adults and £4.95 for children from 4 to 16 years old. Groups of twelve or more people pay £7.10 each or £4.20 for children. The centre is open every day (not 25th December). In summer the centre is open from 9.30 am to 6 pm and in winter from 9.30 am to 5 pm. For more information, phone 020 8409 4400.

1 *pathways* – Stege; 2 *lakes* – Seen; 3 *marshes* – Sümpfe

London Zoo
London Zoo first opened to visitors in 1847. Now the zoo has 651 different animals and birds. There is a new gorilla centre and a lot of other special buildings. The nearest Tube stations are Camden Town (a 15-minute walk away) and Regent's Park (a 20-minute walk away). The zoo is open from 10 am to 5.30 pm in the summer and from 10 am to 4 pm in the winter. It is closed on 25th December. Tickets cost £14.50 for adults and £11.00 for children from 4–17 years old. School classes pay £7.80 for each child. For more information phone 020 7722 3333.

a) Add 'London Zoo' (LZ) or 'London Wetlands Centre' (LWC) in the spaces.

a) _________ closes earlier than _________.

b) _________ is not as expensive as _________.

c) _________ is older than _________.

d) _________'s telephone number is easier to remember than _________'s telephone number.

__/ 4 P.

b) Some children from Nelson School wrote about trips to London Zoo and the London Wetlands Centre. Write LZ or LWC by each sentence.

a) "We saw some birds on a television at the Visitors' Centre." ________

b) "Some of the bigger animals were from Africa." ________

c) "It took twenty minutes on foot from Regent's Park station." ________

d) "We got there when it opened, at half past nine." ________

e) "There was water almost everywhere." ________

f) "The most interesting animals were the gorillas." ________

g) "Our tickets were cheaper because we were in a group.

I paid £4.20." ________

__/7 P.

EXERCISE 3

A trip to London Zoo. Write what these children were doing.

Example: 10.00 am: Steven and Craig – walk / from Tube station to the zoo
→ *At 10 am Steven and Craig were walking from the Tube station to the zoo.*

a) 10.30: Steven / read / brochures at the Education Centre.

____

b) 10.30: Craig / text / his girlfriend.

____

c) 11.10: Steven and Craig / drink / some lemonade at the Oasis Café.

____

d) 11.30: the boys / take / photos of the gorillas.

____

e) 12.15: they / eat / their sandwiches at the Reptile House.

____

f) 12.25: Steven / run / out of the Reptile House.

____

_ / 6 P.

EXERCISE 4

Find a good second part for each sentence. Add when or while to your sentences.

a) The gorillas were having breakfast ______________________.

b) Steven watched a video at the Education Centre ______________.

c) The boys were sitting in the cafeteria _____________________.

d) Craig was walking through the Aquarium ___________________.

e) Someone called Steven's name ________________________.

f) They were running to the Tube station ____________________.

A: he was looking at the postcards.
B: a frog *(Frosch)* jumped off a wall.
C: lots of people came to see them.
D: Craig was talking to his girlfriend.
E: a pigeon sat on their table.
F: a woman asked them what time it was.

_ / 6 P.

EXERCISE 5

Compare the sights in London. You must use all the adjectives in the box in the correct form.

big • interesting • cheap • good • ~~exciting~~ • famous • boring

Example: Covent Garden – London Dungeon
→ *The London Dungeon is more exciting than Covent Garden.* or:
→ *Covent Garden is not as exciting as the London Dungeon.*

a) The British Airways London Eye – Buckingham Palace

b) The Natural History Museum – Guinness World of Records

c) Oxford Street – Piccadilly Circus

d) Hyde Park – Regents Park

e) The Tube – the Docklands Light Railway

f) The London Dungeon – Harrods

_/9 P.

EXERCISE 6

You get this e-mail from Steven.

Hi, Anne and I would like to show you all the sights in London, but we've only got time for one. Here are some ideas. Tell me which one is best for you. Tell me why you are interested in it. Tell me why the other sights aren't as interesting. Here's the list:
London Eye, London Wetlands Centre, Covent Garden, London Dungeon.
Write soon!

Steven

Write back a nice, polite e-mail to Steven. Answer his questions.

Here are some useful phrases and ideas:

I like … • I'm interested in • are exciting • I don't like … • I'm not very interested in … • … are boring for me • expensive • queues • scary

____

____

____

_/12 P.

EXERCISE 7

a) Make pairs.

Example: *book / library*

burn • fire • fruit • palace • passenger • platform • royal • vegetables

______________ / ______________

______________ / ______________

______________ / ______________

______________ / ______________

__ / 4 P.

b) Give a word with the opposite meaning.

outside ↔	______________	begin ↔	______________
best ↔	______________	poor ↔	______________
with ↔	______________	full ↔	______________
get off ↔	______________		

__ / 7 P.

c) Add the missing word.

a) Mind ______________ gap!

b) Stand ______________ of the doors, please.

d) You, Sarah and me: just the three ______________ us.

e) Hyde Park is bigger ______________ St James's Park.

f) I know London like the back of ______________ hand.

g) It's easy to get there, but how can we ______________ back?

h) Buckingham Palace isn't as expensive ______________ the London Dungeon.

i) Steven thinks London Zoo is ______________ best place in London.

__ / 8 P.

GESAMT

___ / 74 P.

09
KLASSENARBEIT

45 Minuten

1/6 Blätter

Lösung S. 190

EXERCISE 1

Reading comprehension

Sally Weale interviewed Declan Galbraith when he was ten years old. This is Sally's article.

1.

A lot of child stars are very busy, so they don't have enough time for games and fun. They can't do the things that most children do. They can lose friends because they are famous. When they are older, some of them have big problems: they use drugs, drink alcohol or steal from shops.

2.

But Declan isn't like that. His bedroom in their house in Hoo, a small town in Kent, looks like any ten-year-old boy's bedroom. There are football posters on the wall – he's a fan of Arsenal and Celtic – and he collects football cards. He thinks his new PlayStation 2 is great; and his favourite television programme *(Sendung)* is *The Simpsons*. What meals does he like best? Pizza and spaghetti. And what does he want for Christmas?
Some new computer games. No, he really isn't like a star.

3.

But when he sings, you can hear at once that he has a wonderful voice, as clear as a bell *(Glocke)*. His first album is coming out today, and if it is a success, he could soon be the youngest singer in the charts.

4.

His parents, Siobhan and Alec, know that life can be difficult for child stars, so they make Declan's life as normal as they can. They think it's OK if Declan is doing something he loves – and he really loves singing. He practises seriously for one hour every day, but he sings around the house, too. And when he isn't singing, he's listening to a song in his head.

5.

Declan hasn't just got a good voice. He also has 'character'. He has dark hair, bright blue eyes and a nice smile, so he looks good on stage.
He doesn't get nervous before he performs, he just feels excited.
He says he was only nervous once – when he sang at the Queen's Jubilee in St Paul's cathedral.

6. | |
|---|

It all started at his grandmother's 60th birthday party. All the children wanted to sing for her, but when the time came, they were too nervous. Only Declan sang, and he sang well. Everybody in the family knew at once that he had something special.

7. | |
|---|

Maybe Declan has got his voice and his music from his grandfather, 'Poppy Ben'. He also sang and played in a band, and Declan listened to the band for hours when he was little. Poppy Ben died six years ago while he was performing on stage. Now, Declan is the singer in the family – and he has already become famous.

Here are the missing headings from the text. Put them in the right boxes. There is one extra heading – you don't need it.

- A very special voice
- Declan's problems
- Famous children
- How it all began
- A normal ten-year-old
- Another singer in the family
- On the stage
- Singing – his first love

__/7 P.

EXERCISE 2

Listening comprehension | Track 9

Anne is giving a talk at school about her favourite pop star.

a) Underline the right answer.

a) Declan is a dancer. / an actor. / a singer.

b) His birthday is in summer. / winter. / autumn.

c) He comes from a family with one / two / fourteen children.

d) With his prize money of £1,000 at the age of eight he bought a computer. / toys and games. / books.

e) He sang at an Elton John concert in front of 2,000 / 20,000 / 22,000 people.

f) Declan doesn't play the piano, / act, / sing, but he wants to try it.

__ / 6 P.

b) Anne made a quiz for the class. Listen again and fill in the answers.

a) 'An Angel' was a big hit in England and in ____________________.

b) Declan's mother is from ____________________.

c) Declan sang at the Queen's Jubilee when he was ______________.

d) Declan has sung on German ____________________.

__ / 4 P.

EXERCISE 3

Here are some questions from a later interview. Complete them with the right form of the verb in the present perfect tense.

a) ____________ you __________________ (have) enough time for games and fun?

b) ____________ you ____________________________ (ever use) drugs?

c) ____________ any of your friends ever __________________ (steal) from shops?

d) ____________ many girls __________________ (write) love letters to you so far?

e) ____________ you ever __________________ (hear) a song by Elvis Presley?

f) ____________ your sister ever __________________ (tell) you that you are a show-off *(Angeber)*?

__/6 P.

EXERCISE 4

Things to do before the concert. Ask questions about what these people have done or have not done.

Things to do	Who	Done?
Example: *write some new songs*	Declan	✗
a) buy drinks for the band	Wayne	✗
b) put the lights in the right place	Jo	✗
c) check the equipment *(Ausrüstung)*	Jo and Stuart	–
d) sell tickets	assistants	✗
e) talk to the police	manager	–

Example: Has Declan written any new songs? – *Yes, he has.*

a) ____

b) ____

c) ____

d) ____

e) ____

__/10 P.

EXERCISE 5

Put the verb into the simple past or the present perfect.

Europe's biggest teen magazine ________________________________

(just / bring out) an article about Declan, and now BRAVO ____________

(invite) him to perform live in their big TV show. Other artists like Sarah Connor, Monrose and Tokio Hotel ________________ *(not be)* in that show yet. Declan's new single "Love Of My Life" ________________ *(come out)* last Friday and he ________________ (already sell) 100 000 copies in Germany alone. Last year he ________________ *(sell)* about 500 000 CDs in Europe. Declan ________________ *(become)* very famous in Austria and Switzerland, too.

He ________________ *(never sing)* there on stage, but millions of people ________________ (see) him on German TV in March and April.

_/9 P.

EXERCISE 6

On a fan club chat page, 'lovedeclan' asks if anyone can translate the interview. Translate Part 2 into German for her. Here it is again.

But Declan isn't like that. His bedroom in their house in Hoo, a small town in Kent, looks like any ten-year-old boy's bedroom. There are football posters on the wall – he's a fan of Arsenal and Celtic – and he collects football cards. He thinks his new PlayStation 2 is great; and his favourite television programme *(Sendung)* is *The Simpsons*. What meals does he like best? Pizza and spaghetti. And what does he want for Christmas?
Some new computer games. No, he really isn't like a star.

____

____

____

____

_/10 P.

EXERCISE 7

Schreibe eine E-Mail auf Englisch an einen jungen britischen oder amerikanischen Popstar deiner Wahl (es kann auch Declan Galbraith sein).

- Finde einen guten Anfangssatz, z. B., dass du Declans Musik liebst / dass er der tollste Popstar in Europa ist / dass du sein größter Fan bist …
- Sage anschließend, dass du bis jetzt alle seine / ihre CDs gekauft hast, und dass du in seinem / ihrem letzten Konzert in Berlin dabei warst.
- Erwähne, dass du vorne warst.
- Frage, ob er / sie dich gesehen hat.
- Sag ihm / ihr, was du anhattest (past progressive!)
- Finde einen guten Schlusssatz, z. B. gute Wünsche für sein nächstes Konzert / dass du ihn im Fernsehen am Wochenende sehen wirst / seine neue CD kaufen wirst …

__ /14 P.

EXERCISE 8

Words for people.

a) Joanna plays the guitar. She's a guitar **p**__________ in the school band.

b) Andy plays the drums. He's the **d**____________ in the band.

c) Paul's mum is pointing to Paul on the stage.

She's saying: That's my **s**____.

d) She always travels to work on the 54 bus. She's a regular

p________________.

e) Andy doesn't do well in spelling tests. He isn't a very good

s____________.

f) A famous artist is judging the pictures in the art competition.

She's the **j**________.

__ /6 P.

GESAMT

__ /72 P.

10

KLASSENARBEIT

45 Minuten

1/6 Blätter

Lösung S. 193

EXERCISE 1

Reading comprehension

Choose the best sport / activity / club for each person. There are more clubs than people.

A Are you happiest when you're on stage? Do you enjoy role play? The Youth Theatre is just waiting for people like you. Come along on a Thursday evening and join in the fun.

B Come to the canoeing club and have fun in and on the water. You must be a good swimmer to join the club.

C Do you like watching 'Holiday on Ice'? Have you always wanted to do the same? Well, here's your chance. The ice-skating centre is open all through the winter.
And don't forget – it's cheaper if you join the club.

D Here you can work out your own fitness programme.
First we explain the equipment to you and tell you what you need.
Then we let you get on with it.

E If you can't swim, don't worry. We have courses where you can learn to swim. There are courses for kids, courses for the over-60s and evening courses for working people. There are courses for swimmers, too.
If you want to be a better swimmer, this is also the right club for you.

F If you like aerobics, this is the club for you. Just bring some sports clothes and a pair of trainers, and off you go!

G Orienteering is one of the most exciting sports there is. If you like a challenge and you don't get lost easily, this is just the right activity for you.

H You can do all sorts of arts and crafts here. We have a big workshop with a lot of equipment. Do you enjoy creating exciting new forms and working with different colours?
If the answer is yes, then – join the club!

I You may think that judo is an aggressive sport, but it isn't. It just helps you to look after yourself if anybody is aggressive to you. Come to the club and find out more.

J You've been on a bungee ride and you weren't scared? Maybe you've done some abseiling on school camp, and liked it? Then rock climbing could be just your sport. Try it and see!

	Club
James likes to be outside in the fresh air. He often goes for walks in the hills with friends. They always give him the map and the compass, because he can find his way better than most people.	☐
Pat is a bit overweight and she wants to get fit. She doesn't like group activities like dancing or aerobics. She would like a club where there is lots of equipment and you can do your own keep-fit activities.	☐
Lea isn't really interested in sports. In her free time she dyes clothes or goes around art galleries. She makes things, too. Last autumn she made a kite for her little brother.	☐
Peter loves boats, and his uncle sometimes takes him sailing. Although he's a good swimmer, he always wears a life-jacket, of course. He hasn't got enough money to go sailing every week, but that's all right. Any sort of boat is fine.	☐
Sarah often goes home in the dark. What if somebody comes up to her late at night and starts to make trouble? She isn't aggressive, but she wants to learn how to fight, for her own safety.	☐
Alison goes in-line skating in the summer months. But in the winter the roads are wet and dirty, so she gives it up from November to March. She's looking for something else to do, but she doesn't really want to do anything very different.	☐
Gavin was in the drama club at school. He's not a bad actor, and he has already performed in front of large crowds of people. Now he's left school, he's looking for a club where he can act.	☐

_ / 14 P.

EXERCISE 2

Listening comprehension | Track 10

You're going to hear a mother and a doctor's assistant on the phone.

Fill in the form for the doctor's assistant.
Write short answers, e.g.: No / Yesterday morning / 37.5°

a) Name: ____________________ Anderson

b) How old?

c) What's the problem?

d) What's his temperature now?

e) When did it start?

f) Is he eating?

g) Is he drinking enough?

h) Stomach ache?

i) Headache?

j) Has he been sick? How many times?

k) Has he got any pain? Where?

____________________ ____________________ ____________________

l) Time of doctor's visit:

_ / 12 P.

EXERCISE 3

Ask questions with *who*, *what* or *which*. Be careful, the question word can be either subject or object in the sentence.

a) Peter – love ______________________________?
– He loves boats.

b) sailing – him – take – sometimes ______________________________?
– His uncle sometimes takes him sailing.

c) make – Lea – for her little brother ______________________________?
– Lea made a kite for her little brother, not a cake.

d) karate or judo – exciting – be ______________________________?
– I think karate is more exciting than judo.

e) happen – to Sarah – can ______________________________?
– Someone can bully her when she comes home in the dark.

f) not want – fit and healthy – be ______________________________?
– I'm sure everbody wants to be fit and healthy.

__/12 P.

EXERCISE 4

Choose a good verb and write the sentence again with an adverb.

Example: Gavin is nervous. → *He acts / performs nervously.*

not fight • skate • swim • dance • find • look at

a) James is a clever path-finder. ______________________________

b) Sarah isn't aggressive. ______________________________

c) Alison is very fast. ______________________________

d) Peter is a good swimmer. ______________________________

e) Pat is a bit shy. ______________________________

f) Lea is very quiet in front of pictures. ______________________________

__/12 P.

EXERCISE 5

Compare Sarah, James and Pat. Write four sentences and use each of these adverbs once:

fast • well • beautifully • hard.

	dance	spell	read	practise	draw
Sarah	+++	++	+++	+	+++
James	++	+++	+	+++	++
Pat	+	+	++	++	+

Example: *Pat dances well, but James dances better and Sarah dances best.*

a) ______________________________

b) ______________________________

c) ______________________________

d) ______________________________ __/8 P.

EXERCISE 6

Choose one of the clubs in the reading exercise and write an e-mail to the club.

You would like to join the club. Say how old you are. Say why you want to join. Ask about the day of the week. Ask what time the activity starts and finishes. Ask about the place and public transport. Find a good sentence to finish the e-mail.

Start like this:

Dear Mr Smith,

My name is ______________________ *, and I'm* __________

____

______________________________ __/12 P.

EXERCISE 7

Choose the right word for the sentence.

a) Sarah is sad because her pet hamster *dyed / died* in the night.

b) Who *threw / through* this ball?

c) Let's lie in the *sun / son* while the weather is good.

d) In the last match Paul *felt / fell* over and hurt his leg.

e) He *heard / hurt* his leg badly.

f) You must *weigh / way* the flour and the sugar.

_/6 P.

EXERCISE 8

Label the parts of the body.

_/12 P.

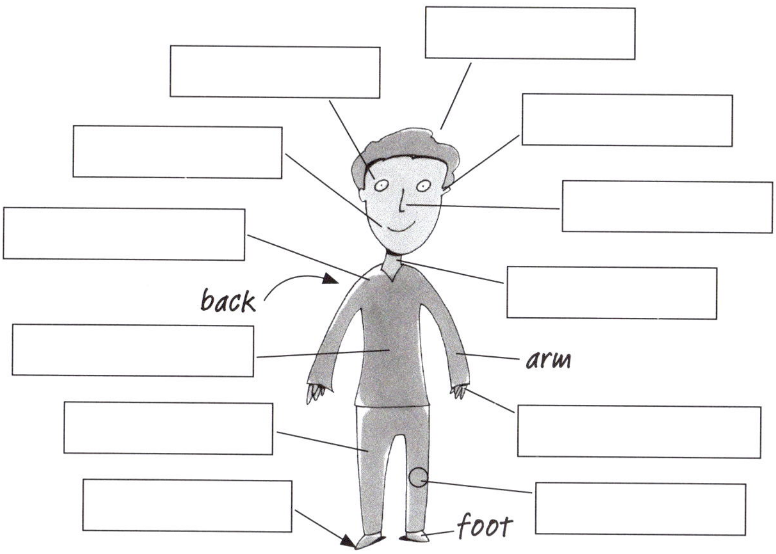

GESAMT

__/88 P.

11

KLASSENARBEIT

45 Minuten

1/5 Blätter

Lösung S. 196

EXERCISE 1

Reading comprehension

Everyone in class 8UW is doing a geography project. Rachel's project is about Shetland. Rachel has started her project. This is what she has written so far.

A ______________________

Why do I want to write about Shetland? Well, I love Shetland ponies, so I've read a lot about it and I think it's a fantastic place, although I must say I've never been there. Shetland is really more than a hundred islands. People live on fifteen of them. There are lots of sea birds and sea animals there. It's a very green place, but there aren't many trees.

B ______________________

Shetland is about 150 kilometres north east of Scotland and 598 miles, or 960 kilometres, north of London. It lies just 01° west of the Greenwich Time Line, but it is only 400 miles (643 kilometres) south of the Arctic Circle. That means that it has 19 hours of daylight in June and July. Of course, in winter it's very dark. The sunniest and driest time of year is between April and August, but it is always windy. Shetland is in the North Sea, so fishing and the oil industry are important for the people there.

C ______________________

You can get to Shetland by air from Aberdeen and other towns in Scotland all year round. In the summer you can also fly directly from London Stansted. There are car ferries from Scotland and from Scandinavia. There are bridges and ferries between the islands, so it is easy to get around. The largest town in Shetland is Lerwick. Only 8,000 people live there, so although it is the largest town, it isn't really very big.

D ______________________

The first people on the islands were the Picts, but they didn't survive after the Vikings arrived from the north. Today you can see a lot of old ruins where people lived hundreds and even thousands of years ago. In the 8th century the Picts dug a hole for a box of silver treasure. They wanted to hide it from the Vikings. A schoolboy found it in 1958. The treasure is in a museum in Edinburgh now, but there is a model of it on St Ninian's Isle, where it lay until about fifty years ago.
Perhaps there is more treasure on Shetland – who knows?

E

There are thousands of sheep on Shetland, and the islands are famous for their soft, warm sweaters in traditional patterns *(Muster)*. But I really want to write about my favourite animals, the Shetland ponies. If you go to Shetland, you will see these ponies everywhere – at the side of the road, on the hills .... They live in the wild and they go where they want to, but they all have owners on the islands. They are very small – between 28 and 42 inches high (70–105 cm). There have been ponies on the islands for over twelve centuries. They have always been work horses, and in the 19th century, people took a lot of them away to England to work in coal mines *(Kohlebergwerk)*. That's why you can often see Shetland ponies here in England.

a) Rachel needs some headings for her text. Choose the best ones from the list and put them in the right boxes.

- A green island
- Ponies
- Sweaters
- Greenwich Time Line
- Travel
- History
- Geography and weather

__/5 P.

b) Rachel would like to go on holiday with her family to Shetland. Which part of the text (A–E) will be most interesting for each person?

a) ___ Rachel's brother Jack is interested in pirates and treasure.

b) ___ Her sister Liz likes big cities.

c) ___ Her dad wants to know if he can take his car there.

d) ___ Her mum often makes her own clothes and is always looking for ideas.

__/4 P.

EXERCISE 2

Listening comprehension | Track 11

You are on the car ferry from Amsterdam to Newcastle. It's early in the morning. Suddenly, a voice comes out of a speaker on the wall. Your family are asleep, but that's okay. **You can answer their questions.**

a) What time is it now? ______________________

b) Where is the breakfast room? – Deck ___________ at the

_____________ of the ship.

c) When does the cafeteria open? ______________________

d) What time can we go to the car? ______________________

e) What was that about the cabin? – We mustn't ___________________ in the cabin.

_/6 P.

EXERCISE 3

Put in the right possessive pronoun: *mine, yours, his, hers, ours, theirs*.

a) Rachel had some books about the Shetland Islands. But they weren't

_____________, they were from the school library.

b) Her brother Jack gave her a map of Shetland and he told her: "Don't

forget, this map is _____________ and not _____________.
And I want it back when you've finished your project."

c) Some pupils were working (in a group) on a different project.

_____________ was about the Outer Hebrides.

d) 'On your islands there are lots of ponies, but on _____________ you can watch interesting birds', they said.

e) One day Rachel also needed Jack's laptop. So he played games on their

father's computer until _____________ he got _____________ back.

_/6 P.

EXERCISE 4

This is the news from Radio Scotland for the Outer Hebrides.
Make sentences with *will* or *won't*.

a) The Irish group *Clannad* ***(give)*** a concert on the Isle of Lewis.

____

b) But we are sorry to announce that Noel Duggan ***(be)*** with the band, because he is ill.

____

c) The Lewis Highland Games ***(begin)*** on July 14, but one day later, on July 15.

____

d) Good news for air travellers: Stornoway Airport ***(open)*** again next week.

____

e) Next month, Stornoway Museum ***(show)*** some Viking equipment. Don't miss it.

____

f) If you can't come, don't worry. There ***(be)*** some pictures on the website.

____

That's all for now. You are listening to BBC Radio Scotland.

__/9 P.

EXERCISE 5

Will* or *going to?

a) This year Rachel and her family ______________ ***(spend)*** their holidays on the Shetland islands.

b) Rachel hopes that she ______________ ***(see)*** lots of Shetland ponies.

c) And she is sure that she ______________ ***(be)*** a perfect guide for her family.

d) On the first day she ______________ ***(take)*** them to St Ninian's Isle for the Picts' treasure.

e) And she says that she ______________ ***(look for)*** more treasure on that island.

f) Liz thinks that it ______________ ***(be)*** a very boring holiday.

__/6 P.

EXERCISE 6

You are on holiday in Shetland and you've bought these three postcards. Choose one of them and write a postcard to an English friend or aunt, uncle etc. Write about yesterday, today and your plans for tomorrow. Find a good sentence to finish the postcard.

Start like this: *Dear …,*

We're having …

_/14 P.

EXERCISE 7

Sort these four words into the right boxes:

foggy • helicopter • bagpipes • wife

Now add two more words to each box.

musical instruments	transport	family	weather

_/10 P.

GESAMT

___/ 60 P.

12
KLASSENARBEIT

45 Minuten

1/5 Blätter

Lösung S. 199

EXERCISE 1

Listening comprehension | Track 12

You are going to hear some information about the Prospect, an oil platform in the North Sea. Fill in the numbers when you hear them. Write numbers (e.g. 5) not words (e.g. five).

A helicopter takes the men to the platform from Aberdeen. The flight *(Flug)* takes ______ hours. The helicopter lands on a pad just ______ metres above the waves. There are ______ men on the oil platform, and most of them are over ______ years old.

The men don't have any days off *(freie Tage)* while they are there. They work for maybe ______ weeks, then they go back to Aberdeen and have ______ weeks' holiday. Everyone works for ______ hours a day. They start at ______ a.m. or they start at ______ p.m. and work through the night.

There are strict safety rules on the platform. That's because, in the year ______, there was a big fire on a platform called Piper Alpha and ______ men died.

_/10 P.

EXERCISE 2

Reading comprehension

Six sentences are missing from the text. Put the right letter by each missing sentence. There is one extra sentence. It doesn't fit anywhere, and you don't need it.

Andy works for a newspaper. He's going to write about life on an oil platform, and he's in the departures room at Aberdeen airport. A lot of men are waiting there. ... **(A)** ... They are waiting for a helicopter. It's going to take them to the Prospect, the oil platform where they work. Now they are putting on *(anziehen)* rubber suits, because the helicopter could crash into the sea. The men call them 'body bags'. ... **(B)** ... There is a short safety video. It tells you how to take out the windows of a helicopter so that you can get out quickly if the helicopter crashes. Most of the men have seen the video many times before, but they watch it carefully.
The helicopter has arrived. It looks old and not very safe. Inside, it is loud. Most people sit with their eyes closed and nobody speaks. ... **(C)** ... The pilot says that if he can't land, he will fly straight back to Aberdeen. But it's OK – the clouds suddenly go away and you can see the platform.
... **(D)** ... On the landing pad it's very windy, so you almost fall over. Downstairs there is a large, warm room with old sofas. ... **(E)** ... This is where the men can sit when they are not working.
"In their free time they just talk about what they have done," said one of the kitchen workers. "When they're working, they don't talk. They can't hear anything because the machines are so loud."
There is a cafeteria on the platform, where the men have their meals. They don't eat much salad. They eat lots of chips, pizzas and pasta.
... **(F)** ... There is a tiny shop where you can buy chocolate and cigarettes. Everyone is friendly. People leave their cabin doors open, but nobody steals anything.
The oil men get a lot of free time and they earn a lot of money – but Andy says he wouldn't like to work on an oil platform. It isn't very safe; and when you're there, you aren't really free, because you can't leave the platform.

- ___ Andy puts a body bag on, too.
- ___ Everyone becomes rich.
- ___ The helicopter can land.
- ___ There is also a dartboard and a big television.
- ___ They don't look happy.
- ___ They like chocolate, too.
- ___ When they finally arrive at the platform, the weather is bad.

__ / 12 P.

EXERCISE 3

Write the letter for the second part into the space.

a) If the weather is too bad, ___

b) If the men watch the safety video carefully, ___

c) If you don't put on a rubber suit, ___

d) If Andy tries to talk to someone who is working, ___

e) If you want to earn lots of money, ___

f) If you leave your cabin door open, ___

A: they will know how to take out the windows.
B: work on an oil platform.
C: you can die in the cold water.
D: nobody will steal anything.
E: the helicopter won't fly to the platform.
F: he won't hear him.

__/6 P.

EXERCISE 4

What will you do if you go to Scotland?

Example: If I go to Scotland, *I will visit Edinburgh.*

Here are some ideas:

put my hands over my ears • buy an umbrella • take a photo of it • not eat it • buy a map • throw it away • ask somebody • run away • record the music • look at the castle • buy a few postcards

a) If I go to Edinburgh, ______________________________.

b) If I lose my way in Edinburgh, ______________________________.

c) If I hear the bagpipes, ______________________________.

d) If somebody gives me some haggis (sheep's stomach) to eat, __________

______________________________.

e) If I see the Loch Ness monster, ______________________________.

f) If it rains (and it probably will), ______________________________.

__/9 P.

EXERCISE 5

If **or** ***when*****?**

a) The men will jump off the helicopter ____________ it lands on the platform.

b) But it won't land ____________ the wind is too strong.

c) And ____________ it's too foggy at the beginning of their holiday, the workers can't leave the platform.

d) But ____________ the weather is okay again, they'll fly home.

e) Andy will write his article ____________ he is back in Aberdeen.

f) ____________ his boss likes the article, Andy will write more articles about hard jobs.

__/6 P.

EXERCISE 6

Bob works on an oil platform. Write about one of his days at work. Use the information in the reading text and these notes.

gets up 6 am • breakfast / cafeteria • buys chocolate • work / loud / machines • break for lunch • shower • evening meal • goes to bed 10.30 pm

____

____

____

____

____

____

____

____

__/12 P.

EXERCISE 7

Each word in the table (B) has a rhyming word in the box (A).
Write the rhyming words from A in the table. Four words in A don't rhyme with any word in B, and you don't need them.

A

alone • daily • fine • hide • know • now •
short • shout • thing • together • town • water

B

although	daughter	ceilidh	fought

own	ride	sign	weather

__/ 8 P.

GESAMT
___/ 63 P.

7. / 8. Klasse

01

KLASSENARBEIT

45 Minuten

1/6 Blätter

Lösung S. 201

EXERCISE 1

Listening comprehension | Track 13

Listen to the PE teacher. She's talking to the head teacher.
Put a cross by the correct name for each picture. For one of the names there is no picture.

A: ○ Simon ○ Elaine ○ William ○ Jane ○ Peter

B: ○ Simon ○ Elaine ○ William ○ Jane ○ Peter

C: ○ Simon ○ Elaine ○ William ○ Jane ○ Peter

D: ○ Simon ○ Elaine ○ William ○ Jane ○ Peter

_ / 8 P.

EXERCISE 2

Reading comprehension

Three friends are looking through a catalogue of sports clothes.
Sally takes size 12 and she wants a shirt with at least[1] 95% cotton[2] in yellow or pink.
She wants two pockets. She can't spend more than £15.00 on this shirt.
Jane needs size 14. She wants a shirt in 100% cotton with two pockets, and it must be red. She can't spend more than £16 on the shirt.
Susie is small and needs size 8. She would like at least 90% cotton and at least one pocket. She wants a shirt in blue or black. She can't spend more than £16 on her shirt.

Which shirt is best for Sally? ☐

Which shirt is best for Jane? ☐

Which shirt is best for Susie? ☐

A Classic shirt in 100% cotton, available[3] in yellow, black or blue. Short sleeves, two pockets with zips[4]. Sizes 10–14 £14.90, sizes 16–18 £17.90

B Stretch shirt in 90% cotton, hood[5], long sleeves[6], two pockets. Colours: yellow, white, light blue, red. Sizes 10–12 £14.50, sizes 14–16 £16.20

C Stretch sports shirt, short sleeves, in pink, red, white or black. 95% cotton, one pocket with zip. Sizes 8–12 £14.98, sizes 14–18 £16.98

D Sports shirt in 100% cotton, two pockets, short sleeves. Grey, black, pink, red or white. Sizes 10–14 £15.49, sizes 16–20 £17.49

E Classic shirt in 100% cotton, hood, short sleeves, no pockets. In black, pink, red or white. Sizes 8–12 £12.99, sizes 14–18 £14.99

F Sports shirt in 100% cotton. Two side pockets with zips. Long sleeves. Available in black or red. Sizes 10–12 £14.99, sizes 14–16 £16.49

1 *at least:* mindestens; 2 *cotton:* Baumwolle; 3 *available:* verfügbar;
4 *zip:* Reißverschluss; 5 *hood:* Kapuze; 6 *sleeve:* Ärmel

_/ 9 P.

EXERCISE 3

Fill in *which*, *who* or *whose*.

Every year, sports day at Nelson School has plenty of interesting events. At the information desks you can get leaflets ____________ give you all the details about where and when the different activities start. In the gym, for example, you can find ten girls ____________ present some new dances every hour on the hour. And don't miss the basketball team ____________ trainer comes from America. It is one of the best teams in town. Visitors ____________ are interested in the team's trophies can take a look at them in the hall. At 11 am you can see the girl on the football field ____________ goals have become famous. And this is for good photographers: Emily and Jonathan from the school magazine are looking for some people ____________ would like to take pictures of the events.

__/6 P.

EXERCISE 4

Make contact clauses if it's possible. If not, fill in the right relative pronoun.

a) Simon is the boy ____________ usually plays cricket.

b) Sometimes he plays badminton against a boy ____________ is in my tutor group.

c) But today he is playing against a girl ____________ I have never seen before.

d) Elaine is the girl ____________ everybody wanted to talk to after the football game.

e) There was even a reporter from the local newspaper ____________ asked her lots of questions.

f) Sports day is the day ____________ most pupils like best.

__/6 P.

EXERCISE 5

Prepositions in relative clauses. Write the parts in the right order.

Example: our head teacher • the parents • into • These are • bumped
→ *These are the parents our head teacher bumped into.*

a) Here's • to dance • every boy • the girl • wanted • with

____

____

b) you • the team • Over there • is talking • can see • about • everybody

____

____

c) at the moment • is talking • Their captain • the boy • is • a reporter • to

____

____

d) a ball • on • we • The head teacher • our names • now has • wrote

____

____

e) There's • he couldn't find • we looked • when • the little boy • his mum • after

____

____

f) those two • That's • rugby players • ran • the referee • intos.

____

____

__ / 12 P.

EXERCISE 6

Writing

**You are going to a language camp for young people from all over Europe.
The idea is to speak English and have fun at the same time.
Fill in your form.**

Name: ____________________

Birthday (write the month, e.g. 21st September): ____________________

Age: ____________________

The sport that I like most is ____________________

**Write a few lines (whole sentences) about the sport which you like most.
This information must be in your text:**

When, where and how often you do it / Where you do it /
Why you do it and how much you enjoy it / Who you do it with

____

____

____

**Here are some activities which you can try at the language camp.
Underline one of them (not the one you wrote about above!) and say**

a) what you already know about it and

b) why you would like to try it.

rugby • cricket • ice-hockey • American football • tennis • baseball • volleyball • basketball • golf • skateboarding • swimming • jogging • athletics • rowing • abseiling • aerobics • judo

a) ____________________

____

b) ____________________

____

_/14 P.

EXERCISE 7

Prepositions

Use the prepositions in the box to complete the sentences. There is one extra preposition which you don't need.

at • for • in • on • to • to • with • without

a) Have you got any problems ________________ your equipment?

b) John got ________________ the finishing line just before Steven.

c) Don't laugh ________________ the other team.

d) What happened ________________ your glasses?

e) You can't see very well ________________ glasses, can you?

f) They are going to show this game ________________ TV.

g) Are you interested ________________ rugby?

__/7 P.

GESAMT

___/62 P.

02
KLASSENARBEIT

45 Minuten

1/8 Blätter

Lösung S. 204

EXERCISE 1

Listening comprehension | Track 4

An English language school class is on a trip to a museum. At the moment they are still on the coach *(Reisebus)*. Listen to the teacher. Mark the right alternatives.

a) In and around the museum the students will need

○ **A:** umbrellas. ○ **B:** sandwiches. ○ **C:** money.

b) If they want to go into the museum,

○ **A:** they have to put some money in a box. ○ **B:** they have to pay eight pounds. ○ **C:** they don't have to pay anything.

c) Which picture shows the teacher's favourite thing at the museum?

○ **A:**

○ **B:**

○ **C:**

d) There are lists with plans in the entrance hall. The students

○ **A:** must get one. ○ **B:** can get one. ○ **C:** should get one.

e) The students can look around the museum for

○ **A:** over two hours. ○ **B:** exactly two hours. ○ **C:** almost two hours.

f) They're going to meet again at

○ **A:** 11.30. ○ **B:** 12.30. ○ **C:** 1.30 pm.

g) They're going to meet at

○ **A:** the entrance hall. ○ **B:** the toilets. ○ **C:** the restaurant.

h) They're going to leave the museum at

○ **A:** 12.30. ○ **B:** 13.15. ○ **C:** 13.30.

__/8 P.

EXERCISE 2

Reading comprehension

About the museum

The museum is in four different buildings. In the main building there is always a special exhibition *(Ausstellung)* which changes every few weeks. You will find information at the entrance about the exhibition which is happening at the time of your visit.

In the main building (Building 1) there are some classrooms. We often have visits from schools, and here on the first floor the students can learn about different technologies or periods of history. They can do experiments for different projects, and there are always people from the museum who can show them the things they might be interested in. They can also help them to find information and to do experiments.

You can find the restaurant in the main building, on the second floor. It is a self-service restaurant with hot meals, salads etc. There is also a snack bar on the ground floor of the main building.

There is also a show of textiles and clothes on the second floor. Manchester was once famous for its textile industry and the old cotton mills are part of the landscape here. In this part of the museum, visitors can do small experiments to find out more about textiles.
It is very popular with children.

The special exhibition area is on the third floor of the building. You will need a ticket for this area. Although the main parts of the museum are free, entry to the special exhibition costs £10 (£5.50 for children aged 6–14).

Building 2 was once a real station. Outside the building there is a copy of one of the first steam engines, with two small carriages. It actually works, and it runs up and down the tracks. The driver will be happy to answer any questions. Inside the building, visitors can see a nineteenth century ticket office. There are also some large steam trains. You can climb up and see where the driver and fireman stood.

In Building 3 visitors can follow the history of power. You can see a 'horse gin', which really meant a horse engine. Horses pushed a large drum round and round to work a machine. Of course, we don't keep horses to work this now. People also used water wheels. There is a water wheel next to the horse gin. As you walk round you will then see steam engines. These were very important in Manchester in the nineteenth century, as there were so many factories which needed steam power.

Visitors who are interested in the technology of flight should go to Building 4, where there are a lot of planes and helicopters on show.

If you need any more information, the people who work here will be happy to help you. They wear a dark blue uniform.

Scanning and reading for gist

a) What sort of museum is it?

○ **A:** natural history ○ **B:** science and industry ○ **C:** flight

b) How many buildings are there?

○ **A:** one ○ **B:** three ○ **C:** four

c) Is there anywhere to buy food and drink?

○ A: yes, two places ○ **B:** yes, just a restaurant ○ **C:** no

d) In which city is the museum?

○ **A:** Liverpool ○ **B:** London ○ **C:** Manchester

_/4 P.

EXERCISE 3

Mediation

Du befindest dich in dem Museum, das im Lesetext beschrieben wird. Eine deutsche Familie hat einzelne Stichwörter verstanden, kann den Zusammenhang aber nicht verstehen.
Der Vater stellt dir einige Fragen, beantworte sie.

V: Hier steht „special exhibition". Um was geht es in dieser Ausstellung?

Du: *Das weiß ich nicht, aber Sie können* ____________________

V: Ach so. Aber was hat das mit „classrooms" auf sich? Hier ist doch keine Schule, oder? Für wen sind diese Klassenzimmer?

Du: ____

V: Meine Frau interessiert sich für Textilien und Kleider. Hier gibt es so eine Ausstellung, wir wissen aber nicht, wo.

Du: ____

V: Moment mal. Auf dem Zettel steht „zehn Pfund". Wir sind aber hereinspaziert, ohne zu bezahlen. Muss ich noch bezahlen?

Du: ____

V: Mein Sohn möchte gerne Dampfloks sehen. Gibt es auch welche, die richtig funktionieren?

Du: ______________________________

V: Gut. Und hier steht „horses". Meine Tochter liebt Pferde. Ist das für sie interessant?

Du: ______________________________

V: Ich hätte noch so viele Fragen, aber ich will dich nicht mehr aufhalten.

Du: Ja, wir wollten auch gerade wieder gehen. Aber die Angestellten

____

__/7 P.

EXERCISE 4

Add *are / aren't allowed to, are / aren't able to or have to / don't have to to the sentences.*

a) The children ______________________ *(not)* eat in the museum.

b) They ______________________ bring everything they need because the coach driver is going to park somewhere else.

c) They won't ______________________ get anything out of the coach until this afternoon.

d) They ______________________ *(not)* pay to get into the museum but they ______________________ pay eight pounds for their lunch.

e) At the museum they'll ______________________ look around for more than two hours.

__/6 P.

EXERCISE 5

You want to visit a museum with your friend. Make suggestions and choose six of the ideas given.

We could … • How about …? • Shall we …?
Why don't we …? • Shouldn't we …? • I think we should …
Let's … • I suggest we …

a) ____________________ a trip to the science museum?

b) ____________________ go by train. It's much faster than the bus.

c) Maybe Simon would like to come with us. ____________________ ask him.

d) ____________________ visit the special exhibition, too? It's expensive but you can see a space shuttle there.

e) ____________________ bring a packed lunch? The meals at the museum are not very good.

f) I don't have a brochure for the museum. ____________________ check the Internet to find out more about it.

__/6 P.

EXERCISE 6

Use the *past perfect* or the *simple past* in these sentences.
Use the *past perfect* for the event that happened first.

a) As soon as the Romans ____________________ Britain, they ____________________ forts to protect their soldiers. *(invade – build)*

b) The Roman general Agricola ____________________ a fort after he ____________________ the land at the Rivers Irwell and Medlock. He called the place 'Mamuciam'. *(plan – examine)*

c) After the Romans ____________________ the place, invaders ____________________ from North Germany and Scandinavia. *(leave – come)*

d) The population of Manchester ____________________ very quickly in the 19th century. Until then, it ____________________ a small town. *(grow – be)*

e) By 1850 it ____________________ very difficult to find a place to live in Manchester because so many immigrants *(Einwanderer)* ____________________ to the city to find work. *(become – come)*

f) Many children ____________________ in damp *(feucht)* houses when Manchester ____________________ to build new houses for workers in the second half of the 19th century. *(die – decide)*

__/9 P.

EXERCISE 7

Writing

An English school class went to the museum. This is what the teacher said. What did Simon write after the visit? Put the text into the *simple past*.

Listen. You've got two hours to look around the museum. You needn't worry about tickets. You can leave your coats and bags at the entrance hall. Now, the groups are doing different projects, so you needn't stay in one big group, but you must work in your project groups.
You mustn't leave the museum but you may go from one building to another. Somebody in the group must take notes for your project, but you needn't all take notes.
You may take photos, and in some parts of the museum you can do experiments. But you mustn't go inside the old cars, trains and planes, of course. You must be back at the entrance at twelve thirty.

We had two hours to look around the museum. We didn't have to

_/14 P.

EXERCISE 8

Put the verbs in the right places in the *simple past tense*.

suggest • shout • ask • explain • reply • wonder

Harriet was alone at home. She was sitting in the living room when there was a knock at the door.

'Who can that be?' she ________________________ .

She went to the door. It was Charlotte.

'Hello, Harriet. Can I talk to you? I don't know what to do on my twenty-

first birthday. You're so good at parties and things.'

'Oh, thank you,' she ________________________ . 'I hope I can help.'

Harriet thought for a minute.

'You could have a dance,' she ________________________ .

'That sounds like a good idea – but we haven't got a big room at home.

Do you know where I can find one?' ________________________ Charlotte.

'Well, I think I can arrange something for you,' said Harriet.

'What do you mean?'

'Well, my uncle has got everything you need for a dance, you see,' she

________________________ .

'He likes young people, and he's got a big house.'

'Oh, wow!' ________________________ Charlotte. 'That's just wonderful.

Thanks, Harriet. I knew you would be able to help. Let's ask him right away.'

__ / 6 P.

GESAMT

___ / 60 P.

03

KLASSENARBEIT

45 Minuten

1/8 Blätter

Lösung S. 208

EXERCISE 1

Listening comprehension | Track 15

Steven has got chicken pox *(Windpocken)* and he can't go to school.
He's phoning David about homework.

a) Complete Steven's notes about his homework.

Maths: page ______; exercises ______ and ______

English: Write about a ____________________ person who is still ____________________.

_/5 P.

b) Put a cross by the right sentence ending.

a) Steven feels

○ **A:** ill. ○ **B:** well. ○ **C:** terrible.

b) In the maths lesson David

○ **A:** worked hard. ○ **B:** listened carefully. ○ **C:** looked at football cards.

c) Steven wants the maths homework because

○ **A:** Maths is his favourite subject. ○ **B:** his mother is in the room. ○ **C:** he thinks football cards are boring.

d) The problem which is not in the book is

○ **A:** long. ○ **B:** difficult. ○ **C:** a dictation.

e) David wants to look for child stars on Internet because

○ **A:** there are lots of them. ○ **B:** they are very interesting. ○ **C:** they haven't lived very long yet.

_/5 P.

EXERCISE 2

Reading comprehension

Last week Steven's English teacher wrote this on the board: "Write about the life of a famous person who is still living." This is what Steven wrote:

The person I'm going to write about is a famous cook. His name is Jamie Oliver. His real name is James, but everybody calls him Jamie. He was born on 27th June 1975. His parents had a restaurant called *The Cricketers* in Essex. When Jamie was eight he was allowed to work in the kitchen of the restaurant. The cooks gave him some easy jobs. He cut vegetables, washed things for salads etc. He enjoyed himself in the kitchen, and learned a lot. When he was only eleven someone described him as 'a good cook'.

Of course, he had to go to school just like every other child, so he was only able to help at weekends and in the holidays. He had some problems at school because he couldn't spell. Luckily, spelling isn't so important for cooks!

Jamie has always been interested in music. When he was thirteen he and some friends started a band. Jamie played the drums. They called the band *Scarlet Division*. The band split up when Jamie became famous, but they still meet sometimes and play together for fun.

Jamie left school when he was sixteen and went to Westminster Catering College, London, where he trained to be a real cook. He spent a year in France and then worked at different restaurants in and around London. A few years later he had a show on television and earned a lot of money. Soon everyone had heard of him.

In 2004 he started a project to help young people. He chose fifteen teenagers who were poor and had problems, and trained them to cook. With Jamie's help they opened a restaurant in London called *'Fifteen'* and it was a big success. Now there are other *Fifteen* restaurants. There is one in Cornwall, one in Amsterdam and even one in Melbourne, Australia.

Jamie is married to Juliette ('Jooles') and they have two little daughters, Poppy Honey and Daisy Boo. Although his job is cooking, Jamie also loves to cook for his wife and children. He is very interested in healthy food for children.

His next project after the *Fifteen* restaurants was a school dinner project at Kidbrooke School in Greenwich. He said that the children were eating junk food at school, and he tried to change things. A lot of people were against him; especially the dinner ladies, because they couldn't get used to his way of cooking. The healthy food was more expensive, too, and soon the school managers didn't have any more money for school dinners. Some of the parents were angry because Jamie said that the children got junk food at home. But although there were problems, Jamie did make a difference. School dinners all over the country became healthier.

Jamie Oliver has written a lot of recipe books. They're very popular. When you read, it seems as if he is talking to you. My grandmother gave my mum one on her birthday, and now Grandma wants one for herself.

Jamie is now planning to improve the lives of chickens. He says factory farms are terrible and I agree. He wants chickens to have a happier life. I wish him luck!

a) Here are some headings for the paragraphs in the text. There are three extra headings which you don't need. Put the right letters and headings in the boxes.

A: Cricket
B: First jobs
C: Healthy food for school children
D: Life in France
E: A good start
F: Steven's grandmother
G: Success as an author
H: A project for the future
J: The family man
K: A bad speller
L: The rock band
M: Young cooks

__/9 P.

b) Choose the correct ending for each sentence.

a) Jamie started working in his parents' restaurant when he was

- ○ **A:** eight.
- ○ **B:** eleven.
- ○ **C:** thirteen.

b) Jamie had problems at school with

- ○ **A:** maths.
- ○ **B:** art.
- ○ **C:** writing.

c) The members of Scarlet Division

- ○ **A:** practise together regularly.
- ○ **B:** play together from time to time.
- ○ **C:** never see each other these days.

d) Jamie trained to be a real cook

- ○ **A:** in London.
- ○ **B:** in France.
- ○ **C:** in Cornwall.

e) Jamie's project for poor teenagers has now got

- ○ **A:** three restaurants.
- ○ **B:** four restaurants.
- ○ **C:** fifteen restaurants.

f) The school managers had a problem with Jamie's school dinner project because

- ○ **A:** the children weren't happy.
- ○ **B:** the food costa lot.
- ○ **C:** the children were eating junk food at home.

g) For his next project, Jamie wants to

- ○ **A:** improve factories.
- ○ **B:** start a farm.
- ○ **C:** give chickens a better life.

_/7 P.

EXERCISE 3

Use a self-pronoun to stress the subject.

Example: Steven didn't copy David's homework,
he did the homework himself.

a) Steven chose Jamie Oliver because ______________________________

______________________________ ***(want to become – a cook)***

b) When he was eleven ______________________________

______________ ***(Jamie – be able to cook – a three-course dinner)***

c) Did the boys in Jamie's band ______________________________

______________________________? ***(write the songs)***

d) The teenagers in the Fifteen restaurants ______________________

______________________________ ***(do all the work)***

e) Jamie also loves to cook for his family, so his wife ______________

______________________________ ***(not have to cook)***

f) When you read one of his recipe books it seems as if ____________

______________________________ ***(Jamie – is talking to you)*** __ / 6 P.

EXERCISE 4

Complete these sentences. They are all type 1 conditionals with will or an imperative. Put in a comma where you need one.

not buy meat from factory farms • feel much fitter
eat a lot of junk food • get healthy food at the cafeteria •
it/inspire *(anregen)* you to cook a meal • want a healthy diet

a) You will quickly put on weight ______________________

b) If you eat lots of vegetables ______________________

c) If you read some of Jamie's recipes ______________________

d) Don't spend your money on hamburgers ______________________

e) If you want to improve the lives of farm animals ______________________

____

f) I'm sure it will be good for school children ______________________

____

_ /12 P.

EXERCISE 5

Complete these sentences with type 2 conditionals. Put in the right verb form and add a comma where you need one.

a) If people ____________________ ***(change)*** their eating habits there

____________________ ***(be)*** fewer illnesses in industrialized countries.

b) Farm animals __________________________ ***(live)*** better lives if we

__________________________ ***(spend)*** more money on healthy food.

c) If governments in the US and Europe ______________________________

(not support) factory farms countries in Africa and South America

______________________________________ ***(sell)*** more of their produce.

d) Prices ______________________________________ ***(be)*** much lower if

supermarkets ______________________________________ ***(not offer)***

such a huge variety of products.

e) If school children ____ ***(eat)***

healthier food for lunch they ______________________________________

(concentrate) better in the afternoon.

f) We _________________________ all _________________________ ***(feel)***

much healthier if we ____

(not sit) in front of screens for hours.

__/ 12 P.

EXERCISE 6

Writing

Schreibe einen Brief an Jamie Oliver.
Du hast im Internet erfahren, dass er Hühnern in Legebatterien (battery hens) helfen will. Du hast Mitleid mit den Hühnern in Legebatterien und willst auch helfen. Teile ihm das mit. Frage, wie du helfen kannst.
Frage ihn, was er vor hat (going to-future). Frage ihn, ob er dazu Poster hat, die du in deiner Schule aufhängen kannst. Sag, dass es in Ordnung ist, wenn die Poster in Englisch sind, denn deutsche Kinder verstehen Englisch sehr gut. Schließe mit ein bis zwei freundlichen Sätzen.

_/12 P.

EXERCISE 7

Put the words in groups to show where the stress is.

action • advice • arrangement • contact • costume • decide • difference • difficult • disabled • elephant • enjoy • official • paragraph • probably • rehearsal • yourselves

Xx	xX
____	____
____	____
____	____
____	____

Xxx	xXx
____	____
____	____
____	____
____	____

_/8 P.

GESAMT
___/76 P.

04

KLASSENARBEIT

45 Minuten

1/8 Blätter

Lösung S. 211

EXERCISE 1

Reading comprehension

These young people from London have all spent a week in a different part of Britain with a host family.

Karen
I went to Manchester for a week. I'd heard all about the industrial revolution in the north of England with its coal mines and factories, so I expected a black, depressing city. Actually it's not like that at all.
The centre is very modern. One reason is that a bomb exploded in the city centre in 1996, so the centre needed new buildings. My exchange partner plays the horn in a brass band. There are lots of these bands in and around Manchester and hers sounded really good. They were very strict about rehearsals. She had to go twice a week. I enjoyed my time in Manchester, but if I went there again I'd take a large umbrella!

Tom
I spent a week in South Wales – Cardiff, to be exact. I'd heard of it before, of course, but I hadn't realized that it's by the sea. Years ago there were docks in Cardiff Bay, but ships don't go in there any more. We went to a concert of the Cardiff Male Choir – or Côr Meibion Caerdydd as it's called in Welsh. My dad would like it – he's into choirs – but after half an hour I'd had enough. I wouldn't mind going to Cardiff again, but next time I'd like to go to a beach. There are some near there, but we didn't go to any.

Sarah
I was in Llandudno for the week. That's a seaside town in North Wales, with a sandy beach. Lots of tourists from the north of England go there for their holidays. Snowdon, the highest mountain in England and Wales, is not far away but we didn't go there. We did visit Conwy Castle. That was an experience! I expected quite a small castle, but when I saw Conwy Castle I realized that it is very, very big. I sent postcards of it to all my friends. While I was in Llandudno I heard some people who were speaking Welsh. I didn't understand a word! But my exchange partner has to learn it at school. She can understand some Welsh but she says she can't really speak it. If they didn't teach Welsh in schools it would probably die out, and that would be sad.

Tony
I went to Chester. It's an old Roman town in the north-west of England. Many of the towns in England have some kind of Roman history, but in Chester you can really see it. We walked along the top of the old walls. They've also created an old Roman street as it would have been in those

times. And of course there's the Dewa Centre, an interactive museum all about Roman Britain. History isn't my fave subject at school, but I got quite interested in it while I was in Chester.

Rebecca
I spent a week in Norwich. In comparison to Wales or Manchester it's not far from London, but it's very different. The town itself has got an old cathedral and a Norman castle, so if you like history it's an interesting place. But what I liked best was a boat trip on the Norfolk Broads. That's a region full of rivers, streams, lakes and wetlands where you can see lots of wildlife – birds, butterflies and small animals. It's a national park. I'd like to spend a whole week on the Broads in a boat. Maybe my parents will take me and my sister there on holiday. I hope so.

a) Each of the young people bought postcards while they were away. Who bought each of these postcards? One person bought two of the postcards.

a) ______________

b) ______________

c) ______________

d) ______________

e) ______________

f) ______________

__/6 P.

b) Choose the best of the five places above (Manchester, Cardiff, Llandudno, Chester, Norwich) for each of these people.

a) Mark Smith goes bird-watching in his free time. His special interest is water birds.

____

b) Dave Hunt is planning a museum where people can actually do things, and not just look around. He's visiting different museums like this which already exist.

____

c) Gillian Jenkins lives in the south of England. She plays in a brass band, but the bands 'down south' aren't very good. She would like to hear a really good band.

____

d) Alan Brent likes hill walking. He also enjoys climbing mountains but he hasn't got much money. A holiday in the Alps would be too expensive.

____

e) Fiona Grant lives in London, but her grandfather on her mother's side came from the north of England. She'd like to go there and see what it's like.

____

f) Frank Chorlton sings in a choir in London. It's a mixed choir with both men and women in it. Recently he went to a concert of a Welsh male voice choir and loved it. He would like to listen to them again.

____

g) Dorothy Pyke lives in a small town just down the coast from Bristol. When she looks over the water she can see Wales. It always looks rather grey and foggy over there, but that's just because it's so far away. She wonders what it's really like.

____

h) Tanya Friend is a student at Birmingham University. Her subject is the languages of Britain. She is especially interested in languages which not many people speak.

____

i) Ken Ellis wants to take his family on a holiday with a difference. He's thinking of a holiday on a boat, but he thinks that the sea might be too windy and difficult.

____

_/9 P.

EXERCISE 2

Dictation | Track 16 + Track 17

Write on a separate piece of paper.

The copy machine at Teignmouth Community College is broken, so the teacher is dictating a text to the students.
Close this book before you listen, so that you can't copy any words.
Listen once and don't write 16. Then listen again 17, stop the text at the pause tones and write the text down exactly as you hear it.
Afterwards, listen a third time and check your work 16.

_/14 P.

EXERCISE 3

Fill in an adjective or an adverb.

a) Welsh sounds very ______________________ ***(strange)***. If you want to learn it, you will have to work ______________________ ***(hard)***.

b) About half a million people speak Welsh ______________________ ***(regular)*** at home and with friends.

c) Since the 1960s Welsh has become ______________________ ***(popular)*** and children can learn it in many primary schools today.

d) In some areas of North Wales you can only hear Welsh. But stay ______________________ ***(calm)*** – everyone can ______________________ ***(quick)*** change to English if they notice that you are not Welsh.

e) Welsh pronunciation seems very ______________________ ***(difficult)*** at first, but, in fact, it is easier than English. Learn it and then you can ______________________ ***(easy)*** say a sentence like:

Diolch yn fawr iawn *(Thank you very much)*.

__ / 8 P.

EXERCISE 4

Decide whether you need an article or not.

a) You can "smell" _______ history in lots of British towns but nothing is more exciting than _______ history of Chester.

b) The Romans built _______ theatre and _______ military camp in Chester.

c) In _______ 15th century people built _______ exciting cathedral. But _______ Chester Cathedral is not the oldest church in Chester. There had already been a Saxon church there for _______ thousand years.

d) And if you are tired of _______ culture, go to _______ Chester Zoo.

e) Take a look at its website first. There you can see some great photos of _______ youngest baby animals in the zoo. I like _______ photos of the giraffe best.

__/6 P.

EXERCISE 5

What will you have done by the end of your holiday? Use the *future perfect*.

a) ______________________________ ***(take)*** lots of photos of animals.

b) ______________________________ ***(write)*** fifty pages in my diary.

c) ______________________________ ***(spend)*** thirty euros on ice cream.

d) ______________________________ ***(visit)*** five castles.

e) ______________________________ ***(read)*** two novels.

f) ______________________________ ***(forget)*** everything about school.

__/9 P.

EXERCISE 6

Writing

Suche einen der fünf Orte im Lesetext aus, den du gerne besuchen möchtest. Schreibe eine E-Mail an die Person von ‚deinem' Text (z. B. an Sarah, wenn du Llandudno aussuchst).

- Beginne mit einem freundlichen Satz.
- Sag, warum du diesen Ort ausgesucht hast.
- Beschreibe einen Unterschied oder eine Ähnlichkeit mit deinem Heimatort.
- Frage, warum die Person diesen Ort aussuchte.
- Frage, was für Freizeitmöglichkeiten es dort gibt.
- Frage nach der besten Jahreszeit für einen Besuch dort.
- Ende mit einem freundlichen Satz.

__/16 P.

EXERCISE 7

Add the missing words.

at • does • her • his • in • makes • of • on • to • with • your

a) The Browns never stay in one place for very long. They're always ____________ the move.

b) When Mr Brown gets a job in another town, his wife ____________ the decision about where to live.

c) Mr Brown usually goes to the new place on ____________ own for a few weeks before the family comes.

d) He says to his wife: Don't hurry. Take ____________ time.

e) While they're moving house, the children try to help, but they often get ____________ the way.

f) When they get tired ____________ helping, they start to take toys out of the boxes and play with them.

g) 'Never mind,' thinks Mrs Brown. '____________ least they aren't babies any more.'

h) Mr Brown is at work most of the time, so his wife has to deal ____________ the day-to-day problems of moving.

__ / 8 P.

GESAMT

___ / 76 P.

05
KLASSENARBEIT

45 Minuten

1/8 Blätter

Lösung S. 214

EXERCISE 1

Listening comprehension | Track 18

The Templetons have got an answering machine. You will hear the messages which were recorded last Thursday.

a) **Who's who?**
The people in the Templeton family are Debbie, Sandra, Marcus and Robert.
There's a father, a mother and two children aged 16 and 11. Fill in the names here:

	Father	Mother	Son	Daughter
Name				

_/2 P.

b) **Put a cross by the most important part of the message.**

a) *Message for Debbie*

- ○ **A:** Sarah won't be at the playground this evening.
- ○ **B:** Sarah's uncle is coming from Canada.
- ○ **C:** Sarah will see Debbie tomorrow.

b) *Message for Sandra*

- ○ **A:** There's been a problem with a pipe.
- ○ **B:** Tom is dealing with the problem.
- ○ **C:** Sandra has to phone some children.

c) *Second message for Sandra*

- ○ **A:** Jenny tried to call her at work.
- ○ **B:** Sandra should phone back.
- ○ **C:** It's about a tennis game.

d) *Message for Marcus*

- ○ **A:** Marcus never has his mobile on.
- ○ **B:** Gavin wants him to bring his guitar tonight.
- ○ **C:** Gavin will see Marcus tonight.

e) *Message for Robert*

- ○ **A:** A meeting was planned for 9 am tomorrow.
- ○ **B:** The meeting is at 8.30 tomorrow.
- ○ **C:** Robert and Peter's Japanese visitors are leaving early.

_/5 P.

EXERCISE 2

Reading comprehension

Here are some messages or parts of messages that have been written by members of the Templeton family.

A: Mum, Gone to Gavin's. Home for tea. Got my mobile. Marcus

B: … thank you for the book you sent me for my birthday.
I haven't started it yet but it looks interesting. … love,
Debbie
PS Do you like the stamp, Grandad? I chose it specially for you.

C: Have 2 work l8, back 7.30 pm. Have T wthout me. CU l8r R

D: Hello Jim,
Thanks for the address list. I'm afraid there's a mistake in your data.
Our address is Boulton Street with a -u-, not Bolton as you've got it.
See you on Saturday,
Sarah.

E: Gavin, Y Rn't U @ home? I'm w8ing @ yr door, no 1 in! M

F: Marcus, Debbie, I'll be out till 8 pm and Dad will be late, too.
Do frozen pizzas for yourselves. Phone me on my mobile if there's a problem.
Love, Mum.

G: Hi, Karen! Thanks for the invitation to your party. Yes, I'd love to come.
I know where you live but Mum wants to know your exact address.
Can you mail it to me? See you at school.
Love, Debbie xxx.

a) There are different types of messages above. Put a cross in the right box for each message.

	letter	e-mail	text message	note on the table
A				
B				
C				
D				
E				
F				
G				

__/7 P.

b) Erkläre die Texte auf Deutsch. Verwende ganze Sätze.

A: Marcus ist ______________________________

____

B: Debbie hat ein ______________ zum ______________ bekommen.

Sie ______________________________

____

____

C: Der Vater ______________________________

____

____

D: Sandra bedankt sich ______________________________

____

____

E: Marcus will wissen, ______________________________

____

F: Die Mutter ______________________________

____

____

____

G: Debbie ______________________________

____

____

____

_/7 P.

EXERCISE 3

Say if it's a passive (P) or an active (A) sentence. Write the letter in the space by each sentence.

a) ___ The problem will be dealt with.

b) ___ There won't be any judo tonight.

c) ___ Sandra has just listened to her phone messages.

d) ___ Marcus' mobile has not been on.

e) ___ The pizza has to be eaten soon.

f) ___ The meeting was planned for nine o'clock.

g) ___ Letters aren't written any more.

h) ___ Text messages by young people are sometimes hard to understand.

_ / 4 P.

EXERCISE 4

Put these active sentences into the passive. Use the by-agent only if the person is important.

a) Robert E. Kahn invented the Internet.

____

b) But some years before, Leonard Kleinrock had written an important book.

____

c) He described how people could send messages from one computer to another.

He described how ________________________________

d) After that Kahn developed a language for computer communication.

____

e) At first the US army used the new technology.

____

f) Later they spent a lot of money on more research.

____

g) Today millions of people use the Internet every day.

____

__/14 P.

EXERCISE 5

Rewrite the sentences and use the personal passive.
Do not use a by-agent.

a) Grandma gave Debbie a book for her birthday.

Debbie was … ______________________________

b) Tom has told Sandra about the problem with a pipe.

Sandra … ______________________________

c) Tom showed Sandra the problem.

____

d) Gavin sent lots of messages to Marcus.

____

e) Karen has not given Debbie the exact address.

____

f) Her mum asked Debbie for the address.

____

__ / 9 P.

EXERCISE 6

Writing

You want a laptop and you've seen these three advertisements. Choose one of the laptops. Write an e-mail to a friend (about 100 words in complete sentences).

- Explain that you are planning to buy a laptop, and why.
- Use the information in the advertisement and describe the laptop you want.
- Say why you chose this one.
- Ask your friend for some advice.
- Say why you think he/she can help you.

ICL300 LAPTOP
Only 3 years old. Works perfectly. Fits into any rucksack or bag (less than 40cm). Price when new: €990. Now only €298.00! Tel. +44-1789-424 336

URL300 LAPTOP
Bought 7 years ago for €889, now only €79. Needs new keyboard. Works well on a good day. 40cm × 34cm. jumblesaleman23@wnet.de

LAPTOP: ECR300
As new, 4 years old but not used much. 33cm × 28cm. Price when new: €1400. Selling for €599.00 Tel +44-1276-116 654

__/14 P.

EXERCISE 7

Vocabulary: 'false friends'

Look at the word next to each pair of sentences. Put a *cross* by the sentence or sentence group where it is used correctly. Only one – A, B or C – is correct.

a) map
- ○ **A:** We'll have a lot of papers so I'll bring a map with me.
- ○ **B:** It's a town we don't know very well so I'll bring a map with me.
- ○ **C:** Don't lose anything. Here, use this map.

b) sea
- ○ **A:** If you want to get to France from Britain you have to cross the sea.
- ○ **B:** We live by a sea. You can walk all around it in about five hours.
- ○ **C:** There are lots of beautiful seas in Germany.

c) action
- ○ **A:** There was an action to make the school playground nicer. Each class did something to help.
- ○ **B:** It's no good just talking. We want to see some action!
- ○ **C:** I know my room is a mess. I'm going to have an action soon.

d) art
- ○ **A:** The earth is getting warmer and a lot of animal arts are in danger.
- ○ **B:** I've never seen this art of bird before. What is it?
- ○ **C:** Bruce is a computer specialist. Art is just a hobby for him.

e) become
- ○ **A:** It's warm now but it might become cold in the evening, so bring a pullover.
- ○ **B:** What would you like to drink? – I'll become a cup of coffee, please.
- ○ **C:** I can't wait for my birthday. I usually become quite a lot of money from my grandparents and my uncle.

f) meaning
- ○ **A:** We didn't agree. Bettina had a completely different meaning from me.
- ○ **B:** Rob had bought a second-hand laptop. I could see it wasn't very good, and I told him my meaning. He wasn't happy, of course.
- ○ **C:** What's the meaning of this word?

g) rock
- ○ **A:** There's a large rock in the garden. We have to cut the grass round it.
- ○ **B:** I like your rock. Is it new? You haven't worn it before, have you?
- ○ **C:** This way for shirts, trouser, rocks and socks.

h) spend
- ○ **A:** There is usually a busker playing at the shopping centre, but I never spend him anything.
- ○ **B:** I just love shoes. I spend too much on them, really.
- ○ **C:** We're collecting for a playroom at the children's hospital. Would you like to spend?

__ / 8 P.

GESAMT

___ / 70 P.

06

KLASSENARBEIT

45 Minuten

1/7 Blätter

Lösung S. 218

EXERCISE 1

Listening comprehension | Track 19

There has been an accident. You have rung 999. Now you are going to hear some questions. Put a cross by the picture which could show the right answer.

a)

○ 1 

○ 2 

○ 3 

b)

○ 1 

○ 2 

○ 3 

c)

○ 1 

○ 2 

○ 3 

d)

○ 1 

○ 2 

○ 3 

e)

○ 1 

○ 2 

○ 3 

_/5 P.

EXERCISE 2

Reading comprehension

Linda plays in an orchestra in Bristol. The orchestra is on a tour of Germany. Here is part of Linda's diary.

22nd May
Arrived here in Germany last night. Very tired but couldn't sleep. I've got my own room here. When I got up this morning my host, Heike (it sounds like 'hiker') asked me whether I wanted eggs or fried tomatoes with my bacon. She thought the English always ate bacon for breakfast and was quite surprised when I said I'd like cornflakes.
We had a rehearsal this afternoon but most of us were too tired to concentrate. Peter has told us all to go to bed early. He can't really tell us what to do, but I'm going to bed early anyway. Can't keep my eyes open.

24th May
First concert last night. It went well although we've all got jet lag. Peter said he was pleased with us. This afternoon we were shown around Leipzig. I liked the old city hall. Martin said Leipzig was disappointing but I didn't think so. I don't know what he was expecting. Maybe he meant the football stadium. Football is all he thinks about.
We leave Leipzig tomorrow morning and then it's on to somewhere called Bielefeld.
That's 314 km so about 200 miles. We're playing at a hospital there and then in the evening in a church.

27th May
Writing this on the coach. The hospital concert went okay. The other one didn't. It started off all right but there was a lot of echo – typical church acoustics. Sometimes the trumpets were playing faster than the basses and Peter was going crazy trying to keep us together. Afterwards some people in the audience said they hadn't noticed. How can anyone not notice?

In Bielefeld we had a free afternoon. Karen, Phil and I went to an open-air farm museum. That was really interesting and not expensive. The lady at the ticket office didn't speak much English so Phil had to try out his German. He's the only one of us three who speaks any German.

29th May
Arrived in Munich yesterday evening. We had to leave Bielefeld at 6 am! It was a journey of over 600 km: nearly 400 miles so it's like going from Bristol to the Scottish border. The coach driver said that we would arrive in Munich in the early afternoon, but there was a lot of traffic on the motorway, so we were going slowly. For about half an hour we had to stop completely. A car driver said there had been an accident. We finally got here at 5 pm. I never want to get on that coach again. We had a concert in the evening but we missed our tour of the city. That had been planned for the afternoon but of course we were still on the coach then.

31st May
We didn't miss our tour of Munich after all. A lady called Hannah showed us the sights yesterday. We went to the Olympic Park. I took some photos and even bought a souvenir although I had said that I wouldn't. Martin said Munich wasn't disappointing. He probably meant the new stadium that the Munich people are so proud of. He and two other boys went to see it. We didn't go with them. We leave tomorrow for Stuttgart. That isn't very far, only about 150 miles. After that there are only two more stops – Freiburg and Basel – then on 4th June we travel to Frankfurt and fly home. A concert tour is exciting but I've had enough of moving around and eating strange food. I'll be glad to get home.

a) Linda's mum told her friends about the concert tour. But she got some things wrong. Mark *right* or *wrong*.

	right	wrong
a) On the first morning Linda's host mother gave her bacon and eggs for breakfast.	○	○
b) Linda was very tired on the first two evenings in Germany.	○	○
c) Martin, one of the boys in the orchestra, thought Leipzig was great.	○	○
d) The church concert in Bielefeld went well.	○	○
e) Linda's friend Phil speaks some German.	○	○
f) They left Bielefeld in the morning.	○	○
g) They arrived in Munich in the late afternoon.	○	○
h) Linda saw the new stadium in Munich.	○	○
i) The orchestra came back home by plane.	○	○

__ /9 P.

b) Who said it?

a) What do you want with your bacon – eggs or fried tomatoes?

____

b) Go to bed early tonight!

____

c) Leipzig is disappointing.

____

d) We'll arrive in Munich in the early afternoon.

____

e) There has been an accident.

____

_/5 P.

EXERCISE 3

Report what Linda wrote in her diary.

Example: I've got my own room here.
→ *Linda wrote that she had got her own room there.*

direct speech	reported speech
a) Heike thinks that the English always eat bacon for breakfast.	*Linda wrote* ______
b) We are having a rehearsal this afternoon, but most of us are too tired to concentrate.	*She added* ______
c) So I'm going to bed early tonight.	*Linda wrote* ______
d) Tomorrow we are going to be shown around Leipzig.	______
e) I don't know if I like the city but it can be fun anyway.	______
f) Martin is such a nerd *(Depp, Langeweiler)* because he is only interested in the football stadium.	______

__/12 P.

EXERCISE 4

Report Peter's commands.

a) Go to bed early today.

He told them ______________________________

b) Please be at the bus at least 15 minutes before we leave.

____

c) Don't be surprised about the acoustics because there will be a lot of echo in the church.

____

d) You must concentrate more than usual this time.

____

e) Remember that we are in Germany and not everyone speaks fluent English here.

____

__/10 P.

EXERCISE 5

Linda's parents asked her about the tour of Germany.
Report their questions.

a) Where did you stay in Leipzig? – Linda's parents wanted to know where I ______________________________

b) Do you like the city of Leipzig? – ______________________________

c) What did you do in the evenings? – ______________________________

d) Why didn't you send us a postcard from Munich? – ______________________________

e) How long does it take from Munich to Freiburg by coach? – ______________________________

f) Do a lot of people in Germany speak English? – ______________________________

__/12 P.

EXERCISE 6

Writing

You are going to have visitors from England in July. Write an e-mail on a separate piece of paper.

- Start and finish the e-mail with a friendly sentence.
- Tell them about two places near you which they should visit, and why.
- Tell them what the weather might be like in July and what clothes they should bring.

_/12 P.

EXERCISE 7

Vocabulary

Fill in the right word.

At the airport … **a)** … was a long queue. They told us … **b)** … take our jackets … **c)** …. We … **d)** … to empty our pockets and … **e)** … everything into baskets. Then we … **f)** … to the gate. People with children were … **g)** … to get on the plane first. We had … **h)** … cheapest tickets so we had to wait until last. There weren't … **i)** … seats free by the time we got on the plane. Karen and I managed … **j)** … find seats near to … **k)** … other but poor Sarah was all on her … **l)** ….

a) it	there	we	g) allowed	had	they
b) we	they	to	h) a	the	most
c) off	out	on	i) many	a lot	much
d) must	needn't	had	j) we	to	in
e) put	sit	do	k) each	the	us
f) must	are	hurried	l) alone	self	own

_/6 P.

GESAMT

___/71 P.

07

KLASSENARBEIT

45 Minuten

1/7 Blätter

Lösung S. 221

EXERCISE 1

Listening comprehension | Track 20

The Smiths, a family from London, have just moved to New York.
Trevor Smith and his sister Anne are telling their parents about the sight-seeing tour they are planning for the following day. You are going to hear Trevor's and Anne's answers.

Find the right question for each answer.

1. ☐ Won't you get wet on top of the double-decker?
2. ☐ Why have you chosen this kind of bus tour?
3. ☐ What places do you want to see most of all?
4. ☐ But then you will have to wait for the next bus for hours, won't you?
5. ☐ Are you going to use public transport?
6. ☐ Isn't such a tour awfully expensive?

__/9 P.

EXERCISE 2

Mediation

Mrs Smith möchte gemeinsam mit ihrer deutschen Freundin Julia Kunze den *Good Laugh Comedy Club* in New York besuchen. Julia hat einen Flyer des Clubs in einem Café mitgenommen, versteht aber einige Ausdrücke nicht ganz. Daher bittet sie ihre Freundin Celia Smith, die selbst Deutsch unterrichtet, sie ihr zu erklären.

Good Laugh Comedy Club

You are over 16 and looking for high-quality entertainment in the heart of the city? Then the world famous **Good Laugh Comedy Club** in Manhattan is just the right choice for a night out with your friends. We are the best comedy club in New York City.

Reservations are recommended, especially for weekends. Every Saturday we feature a special guest, often celebrities known from popular TV shows. None of the other comedy clubs can compete with this.

Admission charges range from $10 on weekdays to $20 on weekends. There is a two drink minimum per person. We offer a wide range of alcoholic and non-alcoholic beverages.

You have always dreamed of doing stand-up comedy yourself? Then here's your chance to learn it within four weeks for only $500. Come and join one of our comedy classes. The award-winning comedian and actor Tony Funny will teach you how to write jokes and present them with confidence on stage. In the last week of the course you will perform your act live in our comedy club. Maybe a TV professional will be in the audience ...

For more information visit our website:

www.good-laugh-comedy-club-nyc.com

Ergänze die Erklärungen mit den Informationen aus dem Text.

a) **Julia Kunze:** Wo befindet sich denn dieser Club? Hier steht ja keine Adresse!

Mrs Smith: Stimmt, eine Adresse steht hier nicht, aber

____

b) **Julia Kunze:** Warum wird hier die Samstagsvorstellung erwähnt? Was ist das Besondere daran?

Mrs Smith: ____

c) **Julia Kunze:** Muss denn jeder Besucher des Clubs Alkohol trinken? Diesen Satz über Getränke verstehe ich nicht ganz.

Mrs Smith: ____

d) **Julia Kunze:** Hier ist ja auch die Rede von 'comedy classes'. Hat das denn etwas mit Unterricht zu tun?

Mrs Smith: ____

__ / 8 P.

EXERCISE 3

British and American English

Mr Smith and his family are currently staying at a hotel, but he is trying to find a permanent home for his family in New York. He is talking to Mr White, a real estate agent *(Immobilienmakler)* on the phone.

Add the missing words (British English for Mr Smith, American English for Mr White). Two words in the box aren't needed.

downtown • gas • an apartment • a flat • in the city centre • subway • petrol • shops • stores • underground

Mr Smith: I would like to rent **(a)** ______________________ with three bedrooms. Can you offer me any, Mr White?

Mr White: Yeah, I'm sure we can find **(b)** ______________________ for you, Sir. Does it have to be **(c)** ______________________?

Mr Smith: Well, a place **(d)** ______________________ would be fantastic, but I guess I can't expect too much. At least the nearest **(e)** ______________________ station should be close by.

Mr White: I see. Actually, I have got something right opposite a **(f)** ______________________ station. That sounds good, eh?

Mr Smith: Let's see … And what about **(g)** ______________________? We don't want to use public transport just to buy a loaf of bread or some milk.

Mr White: It's your lucky day. The place I have in mind also has a lot of **(h)** ______________________________ in walking distance.

Mr Smith: Fine, when can I take a look at it?

__ / 8 P.

EXERCISE 4

Put in the correct verb forms (simple present, simple past, present perfect, past perfect, will-future, present progressive, past progressive). All verbs are in the active voice.

a) Brooklyn ______________________________ *(be)* one of New York's five boroughs.

b) You may know that thousands of people

______________________________ *(watch)* when Brooklyn Bridge was opened in 1883.

c) Before it ______________________________ *(become)* a part of New York at the end of the 19th century,

d) Brooklyn ______________________________ *(be)* an independent city.

e) Many generations of immigrants from different countries

______________________________ *(settle)* in Brooklyn.

f) Presently many artists ______________________________ *(move)* to this part of New York.

g) Therefore some people fear that the rents in Brooklyn

______________________________ *(rise)* a lot in the near future.

__/7 P.

EXERCISE 5

Put in the correct *present perfect progressive* forms and for or since.

a) Anne ______________________ ***(look for)*** her new school ____________ an hour.

b) She is tired because she ______________________ ***(run)*** ____________ too long.

c) Her classmates ______________________ ***(wait)*** for her ____________ 9 o'clock.

d) Some of them ______________________ ***(sleep)*** ____________ the beginning of the English class.

e) Some ______________________ ***(play)*** Battleships *(Schiffe versenken)* ____________ a while.

f) Others ______________________ ***(do)*** grammar exercises ____________ the school bell rang.

__/12 P.

EXERCISE 6

Use either the *past perfect progressive* or the *simple past* in these sentences. Use the *past perfect progressive* for the activity that had been happening before something else.

Trevor liked the double-decker tour through The Big Apple very much, but the present he got for his 15th birthday was even better: a helicopter flight …

a) His parents ______________________ ***(collect)*** information for weeks before they ______________________ ***(buy)*** the ticket for their son.

b) They ______________________ ***(surf)*** the internet for hours when they finally ______________________ ***(find)*** a suitable *(passend)* offer.

c) They ______________________ ***(choose)*** a helicopter company that ______________________ ***(operate)*** for more than 15 years.

d) Trevor ______________________ ***(dream)*** about flying in a helicopter since his childhood, but now his wish ______________________ ***(come)*** true.

e) After he ______________________ ***(wait)*** at the heliport for a couple of minutes, the helicopter ______________________ ***(arrive)***.

f) Trevor ______________________ ***(fly)*** for half an hour when he ______________________ ***(see)*** the Statue of Liberty.

_/12 P.

EXERCISE 7

Writing

Deine Eltern möchten in den Ferien mit dir nach New York reisen. Weil du in eurer Familie am besten Englisch sprichst, sollst du eine E-Mail an ein amerikanisches Reisebüro schreiben, um einige Erkundigungen einzuholen.
Erkläre kurz, warum du die E-Mail schreibst. Gib den gewünschten Zeitraum für eure Reise an (5. August bis 1. September). Erkundige dich nach einem Flug ab Frankfurt (Preisvorstellung bis $ 500). Frage nach preiswerten Hotels.
Bitte um Informationen zu den wichtigsten Sehenswürdigkeiten.
Bitte außerdem um Hinweise auf besondere Veranstaltungen.
Beende die Mail mit einem freundlichen Satz.

Dear Sir or Madam, ______

______

______

______

______

______

______

______

______

______

______

___/14 P.

GESAMT

___/70 P.

08
KLASSENARBEIT

45 Minuten

1/7 Blätter

Lösung S. 224

EXERCISE 1

Listening comprehension | Track 21

Listen to the descriptions of three different states of the USA and fill in the table below.

	California	Alaska	Kansas
a) San Diego is in …			
b) Tornadoes are typical of …			
c) Arctic winters dominate in …			
d) Anchorage can be found in …			
e) Topeka is the capital of …			
f) Arizona borders …			
g) The largest state of the USA is …			
h) The state with the highest population is …			
i) Very large amounts of grain are produced in …			

_/9 P.

EXERCISE 2

Reading comprehension

A
Many German immigrants quickly feel at home in the USA. They like the relaxed atmosphere and the friendly people there. In Florida, they particularly enjoy the good weather. They can certainly do without the grey and cold German winters! But there is one thing most Germans miss in the Sunshine State: German bread. That is why Peter Bauer and his wife Katja opened a bakery in Florida fifteen years ago.

B
Peter was born in 1965. He grew up in a small village near Bremen and finished his apprenticeship *(Lehre)* at the age of 18, but he had already had to help in the bakery owned by his grandfather when he was a small boy. Peter had only had small duties there, such as sweeping the floor. By observing how his grandfather handled the machines, however, he already learned a lot about his future job. Moreover, he became familiar with all the different kinds of dough *(Teig)* used for German bread.

C
Of course Peter would have had the chance to continue the family tradition and run his grandfather's business after his grandpa had become too old for all the hard physical work. But Peter was looking for a bigger adventure and decided to emigrate to the USA, although he had never been to that country before.

D
When he arrived in the land of his dreams he was only 19. He quickly ran out of money. So he had to take on any job he could get. He worked as a dishwasher, stocked shelves in a supermarket and delivered newspapers.

E
One day in 1990 he had a job interview in a German restaurant in Miami where he wanted to work as a waiter. His future boss Katja was from Germany as well. Not only did she employ *(anstellen)* Peter, but she also became his wife in 1993. For both of them, it was love at first sight.

F
Katja offered typical German meats and salads in her restaurant.
The one thing Peter didn't like, however, was the white American wheat bread that was served with it. As he still remembered all the bread recipes he had once learned, he tried to make his own dark, crusty bread.

G

The customers loved it, and so Peter took his chance and decided to open a bakery together with Katja. Ever since, the shop has been as great a success as the restaurant. An old lady from Munich put it like this: "Just the smell here in this bakery makes my mouth water. It's fantastic that we can have it both here: the sun of Florida and German bread."

1. Where in the text can you find information on the following aspects? Check the boxes for the right letters (sometimes you have to check more than one).

	A	B	C	D	E	F	G
a) Peter's and Katja's bakery in Florida							
b) Peter's childhood							
c) Peter's reasons for leaving Germany							
d) the jobs Peter had apart from baking							
e) Peter's knowledge of recipes for German bread							

_ / 8 P.

2. Choose the correct ending for each sentence by checking the right box.

a) Many German immigrants in Florida miss
- ○ **A:** German winters.
- ○ **B:** the German sun.
- ○ **C:** German bread.

b) As a small boy Peter helped his grandfather by
- ○ **A:** sweeping the floor.
- ○ **B:** handling machines.
- ○ **C:** observing him.

c) Peter didn't take over his grandfather's bakery as a young man because
- ○ **A:** the work was too hard for him.
- ○ **B:** his grandfather didn't want him to.
- ○ **C:** it seemed too boring for him.

d) Peter met Katja when he
- ○ **A:** worked as a dishwasher.
- ○ **B:** had a job interview.
- ○ **C:** worked as a waiter.

e) Peter decided to bake dark German bread again because
- ○ **A:** he didn't like the white bread served in the restaurant.
- ○ **B:** the customers had asked for it.
- ○ **C:** Katja served only meats and salads in the restaurant.

_/5 P.

EXERCISE 3

Adjective or adverb? Put in the right form.

a) Katja finds her work very ______________________ ***(interesting)*** as she often meets nice people in the restaurant.

b) She is an open person and makes friends ______________________ ***(quick)***.

c) It is very important for her to see all of her customers ______________________ ***(happy)***.

d) Some people are very critical, however, and don't like their coffee as ______________________ ***(strong)*** as it is served.

e) Then they complain *(sich beschweren)* ______________________ ***(angry)***.

f) Once a customer called her ______________________ ***(stupid)*** because there was a fly in his beer.

g) But even then Katja remained ______________________ ***(polite)***.

h) However, she is glad that things like that do not happen ______________________ ***(regular)***.

_/8 P.

EXERCISE 4

Rewrite the sentences in the correct order.

a) people / few / know / very …

____

… that blue jeans were invented by a German immigrant.

b) forgotten / it / almost / has been …

____

that Levi Strauss had come to the USA from Franconia.

c) There are other German people, too, …
… in the USA / played / extremely / who / important roles.

____

d) the way / Albert Einstein / completely / we see the world / changed

____

e) might / young / you / too / be …

____

… to know Marlene Dietrich, a German actress who became very famous in the USA.

f) another / maybe / but / quite / know / German-American actress / you / popular:

____

Sandra Bullock.

_/9 P.

EXERCISE 5

Rewrite the sentences in the correct order.

a) were born / Fernando and his twin sister / in the 1990s / in Mexico

____

b) moved / but / to the USA / a few weeks after that / their family

____

c) mainly / Fernando and his sister / speak English / today

____

d) at home / but / they / use / Spanish / often

____

e) regularly / go / also / to a Spanish club / they

____

f) there / can see / they / concerts of Mexican bands / sometimes

____

__/9 P.

EXERCISE 6

Use the prepositions in the box to complete the sentences. There are two extra prepositions which you don't need.

at • on • from • with • in • for • on • of • in • at

a) You can come for a cup of tea ____________ any time.

b) Whenever he makes a mistake, his wife comments ____________ it.

c) Although his grades were good, he dropped out ____________ school.

d) ____________ my opinion, you should change your haircut.

e) Look at this house, it is ____________ sale. We should think about buying it.

f) Apart ________________ apples, I have got everything I need for this cake.

g) I don't like this picture ________________ all, it is really ugly.

h) Don't bother ________________ the hole in my shirt, I can mend it myself.

_/8 P.

EXERCISE 7

Writing

Continue the introduction below and write a short pro and con text by using the following structure for your text:

1. first argument for
2. first argument against
3. second argument against
4. conclusion *(advice, compromise etc.)*

Use some of the words and expressions in the box to connect your ideas.

first of all … • secondly, … • finally …
on the one hand … • on the other hand …
because … • as … • this is why …

Many Germans prefer to travel abroad *(ins Ausland)* during their summer vacations rather than stay in their own country. The question, however, is whether this is a good idea.

_/12 P.

GESAMT

___/ 68 P.

09

KLASSENARBEIT

45 Minuten

1/8 Blätter

Lösung S. 228

EXERCISE 1

Listening comprehension | Track 22

Listen to the radio report on a cheerleading festival at a high school in the USA.

1. Check the boxes next to the correct answers / pictures.

a) How many cheerleading squads are taking part in the festival?

O three O twelve O eleven

b) The girls taking part in the festival have to

O cheer, dance and jump
O cheer, dance and shout
O fear, dance and jump

c) What is shown in the picture?

O a human pyramid
O a human tower
O a human triangle

d) The cheerleaders won't perform the stunt shown in the picture above because

O one of them has had an accident.
O it is very dangerous.
O it is a stunt.

e) The judges don't have to

O decide which team is best.
O make sure the girls keep the rules.
O perform a cheerdance routine.

f) Which picture shows the uniform of the Albert High School cheerleading team?

A O 

B O 

C O 

g) Which picture shows a pom-pon as used in cheerleading?

A ○ 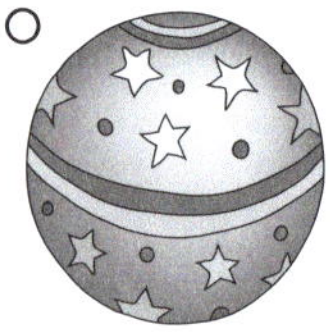

B ○ 

C ○ 

_/7 P.

2. Look at these words. Only one in each group of three is used in the radio report. Check the correct box.

a) ○ audition	○ audience	○ audio
b) ○ even	○ evening	○ event
c) ○ karaoke	○ keywords	○ categories
d) ○ catching	○ matching	○ everything
e) ○ waving	○ waiting	○ saving

_/5 P.

EXERCISE 2

Reading comprehension

Take a close look at the plan of the *Great Fame Football Stadium* and the price information below.

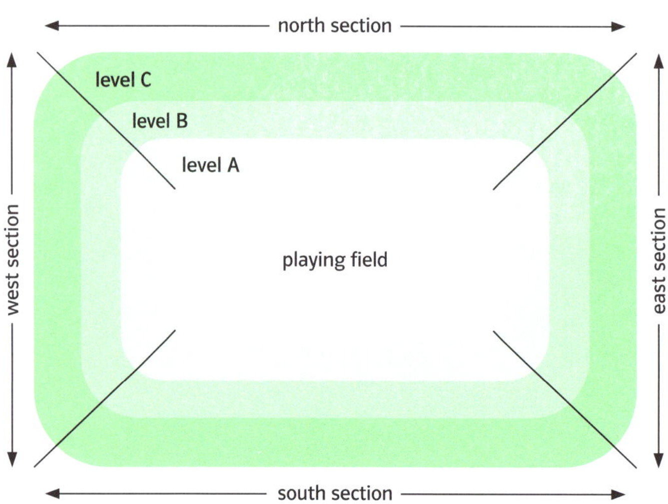

Ticket prices		
	north and south sections	west and east sections
level A	$85–120	$80–115
level B	$65–100	$60–95
level C	$45–80	$40–75

Children 0–3 years: free
Children 4–12 years and seniors (65 years and over): 50% reduction

Special offer:
Family pass for 2 adults and 2 children (free choice of seats!): $150

Ask at the cash desk for:
- detailed price information for season tickets!
- our parking facilities (only $3,50 per hour)

Decide whether each statement is right or wrong and check the correct box.

	right	wrong
a) All tickets for level A cost more than tickets for level B.	○	○
b) The cheapest ticket an adult under 65 can get costs $40.	○	○
c) Children of 4–12 years have to pay at least $30 for a ticket for level B.	○	○
d) If an adult under 65 has got $70 to spend, he can only buy a ticket for level A.	○	○
e) A senior doesn't have to pay more than $60 for a ticket.	○	○
f) A family pass costs more than the full price for two level A tickets.	○	○
g) A senior can save between $20 and $60 per ticket.	○	○
h) Parents with two children under 3 can't save money with the family pass.	○	○

_/8 P.

EXERCISE 3

Mediation

Sieh dir noch einmal die Preisübersicht bei Exercise 2 an und ergänze die Erklärungen auf Deutsch.

Du möchtest dir gerade eine Eintrittskarte für ein Spiel im *Great Fame Football Stadium* kaufen, als dich Frau Schmidt, eine ältere Dame aus Deutschland, anspricht. Sie bittet dich, ihr einige Ausdrücke auf der Preisübersicht zu erklären, die sie nicht versteht.

a)

Frau Schmidt: Hier steht etwas von „level". Was bedeutet das denn? Hat das etwas mit dem Sitzplatz zu tun?

Du: Na ja, in gewisser Weise schon.

____

b)

Frau Schmidt: Okay, klar. Aber warum werden hier „seniors" und „children" zusammen erwähnt? Geht es denn um alte Leute mit Kindern?

Du: ______________________________

c)

Frau Schmidt: Das ist ja toll. Ich bin ein echter Football-Fan und würde mir in den nächsten Wochen gerne möglichst viele Spiele anschauen. Gibt es da irgendein besonderes Angebot?

Du: ______________________________

d)

Frau Schmidt: Gut. Noch eine letzte Frage. Ich habe mein Auto in der Innenstadt geparkt und bin mit dem Bus hergefahren. Gibt es da vielleicht noch eine andere Möglichkeit?

Du: ______________________________

_ / 8 P.

EXERCISE 4

Comment on the situations using a modal auxiliary *('can't', 'could', 'must', 'might', 'needn't', 'should')* with the perfect infinitive of the given verbs.

a) Lucy arrived at the bus stop too late, so she missed the bus.

She ________________________________ ***(leave)*** home earlier.

b) Mike made lots of mistakes in the maths test although he is good at maths.

He ________________________________ ***(be)*** very nervous.

c) Paula had taken an umbrella with her, but the sun was shining during her trip.

She ________________________________ ***(worry)*** about the weather.

d) Liz and Kevin went to the same school, but they only got to know each other at university.

They ________________________________ ***(meet)*** much earlier.

e) Nick dreamed of buying a new mountain-bike, but he didn't tell his mother about it.

She ________________________________ ***(give)*** him the money for the bike.

f) Oh, here's Tracy again! I'm sure she's bringing the apples we need. I wrote her a shopping list before she went to the supermarket.

She ________________________________ ***(forget)*** anything.

__ / 9 P.

EXERCISE 5

Transform the underlined part of the sentences into a *passive infinitive*. You do not need to add a by-agent.

a) Many young soccer players hope <u>that someone will discover them</u> one day.

Many young soccer players hope ______________________________ one day.

b) They wish <u>that a famous coach will praise them</u> for their fast legs.

They wish ______________________________ for their fast legs.

c) They expect <u>that the best football clubs will ask them</u> to play for them.

They expect ______________________________ to play for the best football clubs.

d) They wish <u>that the football managers will pay them</u> a lot of money.

They wish ______________________________ a lot of money.

e) They can't wait <u>until their fans cheer them</u>.

They can't wait ______________________________.

_ / 5 P.

EXERCISE 6

Write down the rules for the *Great Fame Football Stadium* by using the *passive infinitive* without "to".

a) Glasses / should not / carry / into stadium

____

b) Tickets / must not / return / after the beginning of match

____

c) Our staff *(Personal)* / ought to / treat / in a friendly way

____

d) All rubbish / must / pick up / before you leave your seats

____

e) Emergency exits / should / use / in case of fire

____

f) Food / ought to / buy / on our premises *(Gelände)*

____

_/12 P.

EXERCISE 7

Vocabulary: 'false friends'

Look at the word next to each pair of sentences. Check the box by the sentence or sentence group where it is used correctly.

a) desert
- **A** ○ Chocolate pudding is my favorite desert, what is yours?
- **B** ○ While the days are extremely hot in the desert, it can get very cold at night.

b) gymnasium
- **A** ○ The students go to the gymnasium to play basketball there.
- **B** ○ When you have finished gymnasium, you can study at a university.

c) brave
- **A** ○ This is a really brave boy. He always does what he is told and never answers back.
- **B** ○ If you want to do a bungee-jump, you have to be brave.

d) sharp
- **A** ○ Be careful not to hurt yourself with this knife. It is really sharp.
- **B** ○ The Indian restaurant serves extremely sharp food.

e) note
- **A** ○ Could you please note the time of arrival of the train?
- **B** ○ He does not understand anything about music, he can't even read notes.

f) familiar
- **A** ○ The atmosphere in our group was very warm and familiar.
- **B** ○ Her face looks familiar to me. I think we have met before.

g) photograph
- **A** ○ Her job is highly interesting. She works as a professional photograph.
- **B** ○ This is a photograph of my vacations in the USA, it shows a cowboy in Texas.

h) wonder
- **A** ○ The bus driver wondered why so many people wanted to get on the bus.
- **B** ○ It is a wonder that they survived this terrible accident.

__/8 P.

GESAMT

___/ 62 P.

10
KLASSENARBEIT

45 Minuten

1/7 Blätter

Lösung S. 231

EXERCISE 1

Reading comprehension

John McNeal, the manager of the Wild West Museum in a small town in Texas, was very angry. Last night someone had broken into the saloon and stolen one of his best exhibits: an original sheriff's badge from the 19th century. … **(A)** …
After John had put up the new signs that indicated a price change for beverages and food – now everything cost 50 cent more – he had closed the saloon doors at about 9 pm. When he came back the following morning to open the saloon again, he discovered the mess: the wooden saloon doors had been broken open. What was even worse: the sheriff's badge was gone. … **(B)** …
John didn't want to call the police, however. He had the feeling that somebody who worked in the museum might be responsible for all that. … **(C)** … So he decided to talk to all employees of the museum and find the thief himself. He ordered them to his office at once. Nobody was allowed to leave the office until John had talked to them. … **(D)** … He recorded all testimonies. Here are some of them:
Ben: "I have nothing to do with this crime. I worked with the horses till late at night yesterday. Monty, our old mustang, was a bit difficult and it took me ages to put the saddle onto his back. Then he threw me off twice. My back still hurts. … **(E)** … Okay, can I get a coffee now?"
David: "Oh man, I'm hungry. I really could do with a hamburger now. Are three dollars still enough? Well, anyway, it wasn't me who did this. I closed the ticket box a bit later than usual. … **(F)** … Then I went to my Mom's birthday. That's where I spent the whole evening."
Lucy: "The last group I showed around left at about seven. I was really glad when they had gone. I was terribly tired. It had been a really long day, so all I did was go home. I wanted to watch this nice romantic comedy, but I fell asleep right away. … **(G)** …"
When he listened to the testimonies again the next day, he knew he had been right. The thief was a member of the museum's staff and one of his colleagues had lied. What was he to do now?

1. **These sentences are missing from the text. Put the right letter by each sentence.**

a) ☐ This idea didn't appeal to him very much as he liked all of his colleagues.

b) ☐ Yesterday was quite a busy day and the last visitors came as late as six o'clock.

c) ☐ John used a method he had seen in detective stories on TV many times.

d) ☐ I didn't even manage to put a pizza into the oven.

e) ☐ I guess I'll have to go to the doctor's this afternoon.

f) ☐ 'Someone must have used an axe on the locked doors', Jim thought.

g) ☐ It was very precious because it was made of pure gold, which was quite unusual.

_/7 P.

2. Find the following parts of the text and write them out in English. You do not need the missing sentences from above.

a) Letzte Nacht … eingebrochen.

____

b) Der Sheriffstern … verschwunden.

____

c) Also beschloss … Museumsangestellten zu reden.

____

d) Er … Zeugenaussagen auf.

____

e) Ich habe … Verbrechen nichts zu tun.

____

f) Ich habe … als gewöhnlich geschlossen.

____

g) Die letzte Gruppe … ungefähr um sechs.

____

_/7 P.

3. Write down the name of the person who lied.

____

_/1 P.

EXERCISE 2

Fill in the gaps by forming gerunds out of the verbs in the box.

Johanna is a 15-year-old girl from Germany who is staying with the family of John McNeal's sister on a big ranch in Texas.

> to ask • to go • to shop • to try • to help • to take • to horse-ride • to wear • to make • to live

a) ____________________ was Johanna's favorite hobby in Germany and she spent a lot of money in malls.

b) She couldn't imagine ____________________ in the country.

c) She couldn't stand ____________________ walks with her parents.

d) ____________________ on an exchange to Texas therefore seemed like a bad idea.

e) But her friend kept ____________________ her to come with her to the USA.

f) Finally, Johanna risked ____________________ a different lifestyle.

g) On the ranch in Texas she was asked to give a hand, and surprisingly, she didn't mind ____________________ at all.

h) ____________________ and horses became her favorite hobbies.

i) ____________________ a cowboy hat was great fun for her.

j) She loved ____________________ new experiences every day.

__ / 10 P.

EXERCISE 3

Fill in the missing prepositions and the *gerunds* of the verbs.

a) Many people are interested ______ ____________ *(hear)* stories about the Wild West.

b) Some dream ______ ____________ *(sit)* by a camp fire in the evening.

c) Others are crazy _____ ___________ *(travel)* on top of a covered wagon.

d) Most pioneers, however, worried ______ ____________ *(survive)*.

e) They were afraid ______ ____________ *(not have)* enough food.

f) Travelling was especially dangerous if they were bad ____ __________ *(find)* their way.

g) Many of them were looking forward ______ ____________ *(settle)* down somewhere.

h) Some of them thought ______ ____________ *(return)* to Europe again.

__/12 P.

EXERCISE 4

Translate the underlined parts of the sentences into English by using an *object + -ing* form construction.

a) Ben mag es nicht, wenn die Pferde Süßigkeiten fressen.

Ben doesn't like ____ .

b) Er hasst es, wenn Touristen die Pferde schlecht behandeln.

He ____ .

c) Er macht sich Sorgen, dass John den Dieb nicht findet.

He worries about ____ .

d) Er freut sich darauf, dass sein Kollege bald an einem Rodeo teilnimmt.

He is looking forward to ____ .

e) Er ist sehr erfreut darüber, dass so viele nette Leute im Museum arbeiten.

He is very pleased about ______________________________.

f) Es macht ihm nichts aus, dass John Detektiv spielt.

He doesn't mind ______________________________.

__/12 P.

EXERCISE 5

Mr Strict and his students want to visit the *Wild West museum* today. Unfortunately, Mr Strict is not very happy about his students' behavior.

Fill in the correct form of the given verbs.

Ray: "I have to apologize for being late, but this time I didn't forget **(a)** ____________________ ***(set)*** the alarm. The bus-driver had to stop **(b)** ____________________ ***(repair)*** the engine. This meant **(c)** ____________________ ***(get)*** off and onto the bus again for all passengers and took a lot of time."

Teacher: "I will never forget **(d)** ____________________ ***(hear)*** such a fantastic story. I would like **(e)** ____________________ ***(believe)*** you, but I can't. – Oh, stop **(f)** ____________________ ***(chat)*** to your friend, Iris!"

Iris: "Sorry, we didn't mean **(g)** ____________________ ***(be)*** so loud. We just tried **(h)** ____________________ ***(find out)*** more about the museum."

Teacher: "Why don't you try **(i)** ____________________ ***(listen)*** to my explanations instead? I would really love **(j)** ____________________ ***(continue)*** our trip now."

__/10 P.

EXERCISE 6

Vocabulary: American and British English

1. **Search for the American equivalents of the given German words in the word puzzle and write them into the table below.**

   Look for the words up / down and across. Some words might share a letter in the puzzle, some may be written backwards.

_/6 P.

2. **Now write each word down in British English. You only have to change the spelling.**

A	X	C	B	M	F	N
P	R	O	G	R	A	M
C	E	L	T	O	V	D
Y	T	O	H	B	O	E
F	N	R	E	H	R	G
H	E	I	A	G	I	F
K	C	L	T	I	T	O
P	R	S	E	E	E	T
U	V	A	R	N	N	C

German	1. American English	2. British English
a) Programm		
b) Zentrum		
c) Farbe		
d) Nachbar		
e) Theater		
f) Lieblings-		

_/8 P.

EXERCISE 7

Writing

How might the story about the stolen sheriff's badge continue?

Write the ending of the story (about 100 – 150 words).

You can use the following key words to write your ending, but you can also use your own ideas.

- long friendship John and David
- conversation between both
- question of David's motive
- a bet (Wette): theft of sheriff's badge to impress new girlfriend
- David's promise to John

___ / 12 P.

GESAMT

___ / 83 P.

11

KLASSENARBEIT

45 Minuten

1/8 Blätter

Lösung S. 234

EXERCISE 1

Listening comprehension | Track 23

You are going to hear the questions of an interview with Mr Dan Blank, judge of the famous casting show "Everyone can be a star". Check the box by the picture which shows the right answer.

a)

○ **A**

○ **B**

○ **C**

b)

○ **1**

○ **2**

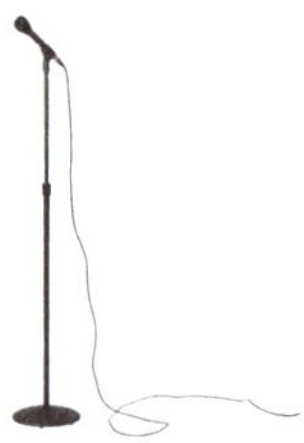

○ **3**

c)

○ **1**

○ **2**

○ **3**

d)

○ **1**

○ **2**

○ **3**

e)

○ **1**

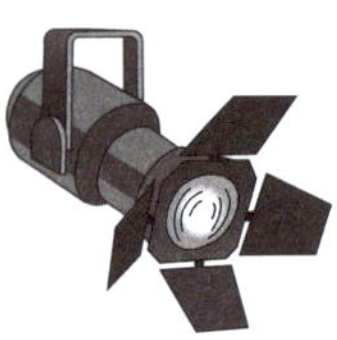

○ **2**

○ **3**

_/5 P.

EXERCISE 2

Reading comprehension

Some of the candidates of Dan Blank's casting show have been interviewed by a youth magazine. You can read parts of the interviews here.

Brian: I think I am a very talented singer, but that Dan Blank didn't treat me fairly. At first I was chosen out of more than a thousand candidates to perform live in the show. Then Mr Blank told me my voice sounded like an old watering-can *(Gießkanne)*.

Lily: My family supported me a lot. I think that's why I made it into the finale. My Mum was always on my side, even when one lady on the panel of judges *(Jury)* said I could never win. I started playing the piano and singing when I was only five, so maybe that helped me, too.

Adrian: What I'm particularly good at? Well, I would say I am a good band-leader, at least that's what my friends tell me. I usually find a way out whenever we have an argument in our band.
A solo career is probably not the right thing for me, maybe that's the reason why I was thrown out of the show quite soon.

Vicky: Getting a professional make-up and all those wonderful costumes – I guess that's what I enjoyed most about being on the show. That's what I have always dreamed of. And I already got a call from a TV producer who offered me a job in his game show.

Toby: I went to a karaoke bar every Saturday evening with my friends. Singing karaoke was nothing I took seriously in the beginning. But I got so much applause from the audience that one of my friends filled in the application for Dan's show for me.
And now I made the third place. Isn't that fantastic?

Who could have said what? Check a box for each statement.

	Brian	Lily	Adrian	Vicky	Toby
a) "My band is more important than my own career."	○	○	○	○	○
b) "Taking part in this show was one of the worst ideas of my life."	○	○	○	○	○
c) "Singing was just a fun thing for me at first."	○	○	○	○	○
d) "I am simply a fashion maniac."	○	○	○	○	○
e) "Music has been a part of my life since my early childhood."	○	○	○	○	○
f) "My Mom always told me she believed in me."	○	○	○	○	○
g) "It seems I have a very good chance of a TV career."	○	○	○	○	○
h) "I can solve any problem within our band."	○	○	○	○	○
i) "I was only chosen because Mr Blank wanted to make fun of me."	○	○	○	○	○
j) "I am so grateful to my friend."	○	○	○	○	○

__ / 10 P.

EXERCISE 3

Mediation

Karen, an American exchange student in Berlin, has always dreamed of taking part in a casting show. She has found some interesting information on the website of a German TV channel, but doesn't understand everything she needs to know. **Can you help her?**

Sommercasting in Berlin!

Du bist zwischen 16 und 30 Jahre alt?
Du weißt dich auf einer Bühne gut zu präsentieren?
Singen kannst du auch noch?
Dann nichts wie los – mach mit beim Sommercasting in Berlin! Die Gewinner nehmen an der bekannten Fernsehshow „Deutschland singt" teil. Du kannst dich bis zum 15. April bei Frau Krach unter dem Motto „Gesangstalent" per Telefon, online oder per SMS bewerben. Gib dazu deinen Namen, dein Alter und deine Adresse an. Außerdem benötigen wir von dir folgende Angaben:

- Kannst du ein Instrument spielen? (Welches? Wie lange spielst du schon?)
- Welchen Song möchtest du beim Casting vortragen?
- Welche anderen Talente hast du? (Tanzen? Schauspielerei?)

Wir freuen uns darauf, dich kennenzulernen!

a)
Karen: I understand that you have to be able to sing well to take part in the casting. But are there any other conditions?
You: Actually there are two other conditions.

____

b)
Karen: Okay, that's no problem. But why is Germany mentioned here?

You: ______________________________

c)
Karen: I see. Do I have to send an SMS text message for the application?

You: ______________________________

d)
Karen: Fine. Surely the organizers of the casting will need my name, age and my address. But what else do they want to know?
You: There are three other things they ask:

____

_/14 P.

EXERCISE 4

Fill in the correct passive forms of the given verbs. Use the *simple passive* (*present, past, present perfect, past perfect, will-future or infinitive*).

a) British rock and pop bands can ______________________________
(hear) on the radio every day.

b) One of the first bands that ______________________________
(love) by German fans were the Beatles.

c) The band ______________________________ *(form)* in Liverpool in 1960, but the Beatles also spent a lot of time in Hamburg in their early years.

d) Their records ______________________________ *(buy)* by millions of fans up to today.

e) After the charts ______________________________
(dominated) by their songs for many years, the Beatles split up in 1970.

f) Even today many tears ______________________________
(cry) because this band doesn't exist anymore.

g) Some fans think that the Beatles' success ______________________________
(never repeat) by another band.

__/7 P.

EXERCISE 5

Put in the verb in the *present progressive passive* or the *past progressive passive.*

to allow • to go • to use • to forbid • to wear •
to consider • to see • to invent

a) Many fashion items that ______________________________ ***(wear)*** at the moment have a strange history.

b) Currently, baggy pants ______________________________ ***(consider)*** a basic piece of clothing by many boys, especially those who like Rap or HipHop.

c) Many say that baggy pants ______________________________ ***(invent)*** by gangsters while they were in prison.

d) The typical prison outfit without a belt ______________________________ ***(turn)*** into a fashion statement.

e) Later baggy pants ______________________________ ***(use)*** by Rappers as a sign of toughness when there were gang fights.

f) Nowadays these pants ______________________________ ***(see)*** as a sign of a bad character by some people.

g) Laws against baggy pants ______________________________ ***(discuss)*** in some American states at the moment.

__/7 P.

EXERCISE 6

Put the sentences into the *passive voice* (please use the *by-agent*).

a) Music journalists have written about punk rock for years.

____

b) In the early eighties parents worried about the dangers of the punk movement.

____

c) The police had already dealt with many punks.

____

d) Some punks broke into empty houses to live there.

____

e) Punk bands like the *Sex Pistols* made fun of high politicians *(Politiker)*.

____

f) Today young punks still talk about the early days of the punk movement.

____ __ / 12 P.

EXERCISE 7

The two sentences mean the same. Add the right verb.

a) The hotel room was ugly and dirty. She couldn't accept that what she saw was real.
The hotel room was ugly and dirty. She couldn't ________________ her eyes.

b) I'm so happy about this beautiful present. I don't know what to say.
I'm so happy about this beautiful present.
I don't know how to ________________ it into words.

c) Tom and Sue met at a party. They began to feel love for each other at once.
Tom and Sue met at a party. They ________________ in love with each other at once.

d) Can't you see that I want to be on my own now? Leave the room, Mike!
Can't you see that I want to be on my own now? ________________ out of my sight, Mike!

e) Lisa and Ned shared the household work fairly. One day she cooked the meal, the next day it was his turn.
Lisa and Ned shared the household work fairly. They ________________ turns cooking the meals.

f) This course sounds very interesting, I'd really like to do it.
This course sounds very interesting, I'd really like to ________________ part in it.

__ / 6 P.

GESAMT

___ / 61 P.

12

KLASSENARBEIT

45 Minuten

1/5 Blätter

Lösung S. 237

EXERCISE 1

Reading comprehension

A couple of young people are looking for the right job for their vacation. Look at the newspaper ads and decide which job is best for which person. (There are two suitable persons for each job.)

Mark the description of each person with A, B, or C accordingly.

A

We are looking for a paper deliverer for the months of July and August. You should be a reliable person and take your job seriously. Punctuality should be very important for you.
We expect you to start work at 5 am. We will provide you with a detailed map of the paper round to help you find your way. You will have to walk about 5 miles every day, so you need good stamina. You should be able to work on Saturdays.
Interested? Then call 0500-324-54432.

B

You have good communication skills and know how to work with a word processing program? You are well-organized and have got neat hand-writing? You have got a good memory and you like paper work? You prefer regular working hours Mondays to Fridays?
Then you should apply for the temporary job of a secretary at our down-town office. For more information take a look at www.our-downtown-office.com

C

Mamma Lucia's Pizza Restaurant is looking for a vacation replacement for our pizza-baker. Our restaurant is often very busy, so you should be able to work quickly. Strong nerves and a good sense of humour are equally important. You shouldn't mind long working hours. Our restaurant is closed on Mondays, but open on all the other days.
Why don't you drop by and talk to us personally? (Our restaurant is in Cheese Street 232a.)

a) ☐ Mary is a talkative person. She is doing her first year of business studies. Every Saturday she babysits her nephew.

b) ☐ James has just finished high-school. He is a good runner, but doesn't like to be in the company of other people for too long.

c) ☐ Marvin is not a very orderly person, but good fun to be with. His mother often complains because he is a late riser *(Spätaufsteher)*.

d) ☐ Faye loves fast cars, but she doesn't like walking. She spends every Monday with her grandma and helps her with her housework.

e) ☐ Playing soccer is Paul's favorite hobby. Every weekend he takes part in at least two matches of his team.

f) ☐ Laura is not allowed to work in the evenings. It is hard for her to sit still for more than five minutes.

__/9 P.

EXERCISE 2

Jack has heard about the job at Mamma Lucia's Pizza Restaurant, too. He wants to know more about the job before going to the restaurant in person.

Underline the expressions that Jack shouldn't use in this formal phone conversation.

a) **Mr Fry:** How can I help you?
Jack: Hey dude, I'm kinda interested in the job at your pizza restaurant.

b) **Mr Fry:** Where did you hear about the job?
Jack: Sarah, a buddy of mine, is already working at your place, and she's like, you need more people in the kitchen.

c) **Mr Fry:** Have you got any working experience?
Jack: I dunno a lot about cooking, but I have done a lotta different jobs.

d) **Mr Fry:** So you are not qualified for a job in the kitchen?
Jack: Well, people go, I'm a quick learner big time, so this shouldn't be a problem.

e) **Mr Fry:** I see. Is there anything you would like to know about the job?
Jack: Yes, can you gimme some information on the bucks I would get?

__/10 P.

EXERCISE 3

Write down complete sentences, using a construction with an object + infinitive after the verb.

a) Mr Fry / want / pizza-baker / work fast

b) He / expect / restaurant / be busy

c) He / prefer / staff / use fresh food

d) He / advise / waiters / learn Italian

e) He / tell / everyone / be patient with guests

f) He / ask / guests / try delicious pizza

_/12 P.

EXERCISE 4

Bob is one of the people who applied for the job as a paper deliverer and he actually got it. Before he starts work, he asks a lot of questions.

Rewrite Bob's questions by using the infinitive with "to" after question words.

a) Should I take an umbrella with me?

Bob wonders ______________________________

b) What shall I do if I get lost?

He wants to know ______________________________

c) Where can I sit down to take a break?

He is not sure ______________________________

d) What do I have to do if I am late?

He has no idea ______________________________

e) Do I (have to) work every Saturday?

He doesn't remember ______________________________

f) When can I start my new job?

He wants to be told ______________________________

_/9 P.

EXERCISE 5

Not all young people want to work during their vacations. A girl who took part in a vacation camp in Austria is talking about the other teenagers there.

Complete what she says with information from the box.

youngest girl • go to the camp
last • reach the top of the mountain
best partner • sing with
most interesting boy • listen to
first • do a bungee-jump
only one • make lunch

a) Chris is very brave. He was ______________________________

b) Caro loves cooking. She was ______________________________

c) Lukas is a bad climber. He was ______________________________

d) Paula is only 13. She was ______________________________

e) Meike is crazy about music. She was ______________________________

f) Martin knows many stories. He was ______________________________

__ / 9 P.

EXERCISE 6

Use relative clauses to combine two sentences and form one.

a) Many teenagers own cell phones. Communication is very important for them.

b) The term 'texting' refers to the exchange of short written messages. This is called 'simsen' in German.

c) Extravagant ring tones for cell phones are very popular. These ring tones are often parts of well-known songs.

d) The first cell phone was almost as big as a brick. Its modern version can be put into a pants pocket.

e) There are many family arguments because of cell phones. Their costs are often high.

__ / 10 P.

EXERCISE 7

Writing

Answer the following letter to an agony aunt (Kummerkastentante). Make three suggestions to help Mrs Sunny. Don't forget to begin and end your letter with a friendly sentence.

Dear Mrs Wise,

I'm writing to you because I have got serious problems with my 14-year-old son. He keeps playing computer games for hours instead of doing his homework. Consequently his grades at school have worsened at lot. What is more, he has stopped playing football, which used to be his favorite hobby. I told him not to use the computer for games anymore, but he doesn't listen. It is also hard for me to control what he is doing as he has his own computer in his room.

What can I do to change the situation? Please help me!

Yours
Susan Sunny

__/12 P.

GESAMT

___/71 P.

LÖSUNGEN

5.–8. Klasse

01

LÖSUNGEN

KA Seite 14

LÖSUNG ZU AUFGABE 1

Hörverstehen 1

Höre dem Mädchen zu und unterstreiche die richtigen Wörter oder Zahlen.

Hello! I'm Jean, that's J E A N, and I'm from Bristol. I'm twelve years old. I'm new in Bromley. My friends at Nelson School are Rachel and Steven. I play football in the playground at lunchtime, but football isn't my favourite sport. That's tennis.

Name:	Jean
From:	Bristol
Age:	12
New in Bromley:	Yes
New friends:	Rachel and Steven
Favourite sport:	tennis

Gib dir für jede richtige Antwort 1 Punkt.

LÖSUNG ZU AUFGABE 2

Leseverstehen

b) Kreuze das richtige Bild an.

a) B   b) A   c) C   d) A   e) B   f) A

Für jede richtige Antwort bekommst du 1 Punkt.

LÖSUNG ZU AUFGABE 3

Übersetzung

Übersetze die Sätze und schreibe sie auf.

a) Write in your exercise books, please.

b) Thank you.

c) Now there is one crisp.

d) There's a mouse in my bag.

Gib dir für jeden richtigen Satz 1 Punkt.

LÖSUNG ZU AUFGABE 4

Du bist David. Schreibe einen Text.

My name is David Thornton. I'm eleven years old. I'm not new in Bromley. My favourite sport is football. My friends are Steven, Paul and Rachel.

TIPP

Singular:
is – *my name is*

Plural:
are – *my friends are*

Gib dir für jeden richtigen Satz $\frac{1}{8}$ Punkte.
Max. 9 Punkte.

LÖSUNG ZU AUFGABE 5

Schreibe das Wort oder die Wörter in den richtigen Kasten.

a: unit, bag, folder, big apple, classroom
an: apple, answer, old car, English book, exercise book

Für jedes richtig zugeordnete Wort bekommst du ½ Punkt.

LÖSUNG ZU AUFGABE 6

TIPP

Auf die Aussprache kommt es an, nicht auf den Buchstaben: *a unit*, so wie *a yellow apple*.

Wo sind die Sachen?

a) The book is on the desk.

b) The schoolbag is under the desk.

c) The exercise books are behind the chair.

d) The chair is in front of the desk.

e) Two pupils are in front of the board.

f) An old sandwich is on the chair.

Gib dir für jeden richtigen Satz 1 Punkt.

LÖSUNG ZU AUFGABE 7

TIPP

there is für eine Person oder Sache

there are für zwei und mehr

Vervollständige die Sätze. In Rachels Klassenzimmer gibt es

a) In Rachel's classroom there are 30 desks.

b) … there are four windows.

c) … there are 15 apples.

d) … there are 28 pencil-cases.

e) … there are two footballs.

f) … there is one teacher.

Gib dir für jeden richtigen Satz 1 Punkt.

LÖSUNG ZU AUFGABE 8

Bilde Fragen. Verwende: where – who – what.

a) Where are they?

b) Who is it?

c) Where is she from?

d) What's her name?

e) Who are you?

Für jede richtige Frage bekommst du 2 Punkte.

LÖSUNG ZU AUFGABE 9

Setze ein passendes Adjektiv ein.

a) Football is a **nice / boring / cool / old sport**.

b) I'm sorry, but this answer is **wrong**.

c) Is your schoolbag **new / cool / nice / big**?

d) My school is so **old / boring / nice / cool**.

e) Your jokes aren't funny, they're **boring**.

Für jede richtige Antwort bekommst du 1 Punkt.

LÖSUNG ZU AUFGABE 10

Finde die Personen und schreibe sie heraus.

friend, teacher, tutor, pupil, caretaker, girl, boy, mum

Gib dir für jede gefundene Person ½ Punkt.

MEIN ERGEBNIS

Punkte	61–57	56–54	53–49	48–46	45–40	39–37	36–31	30–28	27–17	16	15–0
Note	1	1,5	2	2,5	3	3,5	4	4,5	5	5,5	6

02

LÖSUNGEN

KA Seite 21

LÖSUNG ZU AUFGABE 1

Hörverstehen 2

a) Anne ist bei Rachel. Hake das richtige Bild ab.

Anne: So this is your shed. Have you got drums?
Rachel: No, I haven't. They're my dad's drums. I can't play them.
Anne: Are there mice in here? There's a funny smell.
Rachel: Yes, there are. But don't tell my mum and dad!

Lösung: **B**

b) Jetzt ist Rachels Vater hier. Welches Bild stimmt?

Hello! You're Anne, aren't you? I'm Rachel's dad. I know you're interested in computers. Rachel wants a computer, but her room is very small, so she hasn't got a computer. And her T-shirts and other things are in her sister's room, in a big wardrobe. Rachel hasn't got a wardrobe. And her desk is in the living room. That can be a problem. But she has got a new chemistry set. Look, there's a crystal here. Are you interested in chemistry?

Lösung: **C**

Für jede richtige Frage bekommst du 2 Punkte.

LÖSUNG ZU AUFGABE 2

Leseverstehen

a) Kreuze die richtige Antwort an.

1. 13 2. Rose 3. in the shed 4. only a laptop

b) Im Lesetext fehlen drei Sätze. Hier sind sie. Setze die Buchstaben A, B, C an die richtge Stelle.

C Have you got your own room?
B She's here in London.
A He's four years old.

Für jede richtige Antwort bekommst du 1 Punkt.

LÖSUNG ZU AUFGABE 3

Das ist Rachels Familie und ihre Wohnung. Setze ein ...

Anne: There's a chemistry set on the desk. Is it **your** chemistry set?
Rachel: Yes, it is. And this is **my** new bed. My old bed is for Jack. It's in **his** room now.
Anne: Has your sister got **her** own room?
Rachel: Yes, she has. But we can do **our** homework in the living room.
Anne: Your mum and dad are nice. Is that **their** bedroom?
Rachel: No, it isn't. It's Jack's room. Just look at **his** room. What a mess!

Gib dir für jede richtige Antwort 1 Punkt.

LÖSUNG ZU AUFGABE 4

Bilde Sätze zu Rachel Hills Familie und Wohnung.

a) Liz is Rachel's sister.

b) The Hills' flat is in Croydon Road.

c) The girls' wardrobe is a problem.

d) Jack is Rachel's little brother.

e) Her parents' bedroom is big.

TIPP

Singular:
*the **girl's** wardrobe*

Plural:
*the **girls'** wardrobe*

Gib dir für jeden richtigen Satz 2 Punkte.

LÖSUNG ZU AUFGABE 5

Bilde Fragen und gib Kurzantworten.

a) Have you got a desk in your room? – Yes, I have.

b) Have you got two bedrooms? – No, I haven't.

c) Has your brother got his own computer? – No, he hasn't.

d) Have your parents got two cars? – Yes, they have.

Was hast du oder hast du nicht in deinem Zimmer? Schreibe zwei Sätze.

e) und f) – *individuelle Angaben, z. B.*
I've got a laptop in my room. I haven't got a sofa in my room.

TIPP

I / you / we / they
have got

he / she / it
has got

Für jede richtige Frage mit Kurzantwort bekommst du 2 Punkte.

LÖSUNG ZU AUFGABE 6

Schreibe vier Regeln für die Zimmer von Liz und Rachel auf.
Verwende den Lesetext (Aufgabe 2) für Anregungen.

Einige Möglichkeiten:
Don't use the desk when my friends are in the room.
Don't take my T-shirts.
Be quiet when I've got homework.
Don't play my CDs when you've got homework.
Don't put your schoolbag in my room.
Don't use my school things.
Take turns when we've got homework.

Gib dir für jeden richtigen Satz 1 Punkt. Max. 8 Punkte.

MEIN ERGEBNIS

Punkte	48 – 44	43 – 41	40 – 38	37 – 35	34 – 30	29 – 27	26 – 24	23 – 21	20 – 12	11	10 – 0
Note	1	1,5	2	2,5	3	3,5	4	4,5	5	5,5	6

03
LÖSUNGEN

KA Seite 25

LÖSUNG ZU AUFGABE 1

Hörverstehen 3

Mr Large hat eine Liste der AGs an der Bromley Schule. Höre Mr Large zu und hilf Steven bei der fehlenden Information. In der Spalte ‚Time' schreibe Zahlen.

Now listen, please, girls and boys. You're all new at Bromley School, and there are a lot of clubs at the school. You've got a grid. Listen and fill in the grid. We've got an orchestra at the school. The orchestra meets in the music room. Maybe you can play the guitar … or the drums …? They meet on Monday at three thirty. It finishes at four thirty. The teacher is Mrs White. Then there's the film club. Are you interested in films? It's in Room B32. It's on Tuesday from 4 o'clock to quarter past five in the afternoon. Mr Watson is the film club teacher. Or how about the Internet café? You can go on the Internet in the computer room.
Mrs Holding can help you. That's on Wednesday from half past three to quarter to five. Or you can go to the cooking club. You can make lunches or cakes with Mr Appleton. That's in the school kitchen. It's on Thursday. It starts at three fifteen and it finishes at four forty-five pm. So you see, there are lots of interesting clubs at the school. But don't …

Name: *Steven Hall* — Tutor group: *7UW*

Club	Room	Day of the week	Time	Teacher
Orchestra	**Music** room	**Monday**	3.30 pm – **4.30 pm**	**Mrs** White
Film club	Room **B32**	Tuesday	**4.00 pm** – 5.15 pm	Mr Watson
Internet **café**	**Computer** room	Wednesday	**3.30 pm** – 4.45 pm	Mrs Holding
Cooking club	School **kitchen**	**Thursday**	3.15 pm – **4.45 pm**	**Mr** Appleton

Gib dir für jede richtige Antwort 1 Punkt.

LÖSUNG ZU AUFGABE 2

Leseverstehen

Hier ist eine Liste der AGs an der Bromley Schule. Finde die richtige AG für jedes Kind.

Andy: orchestra	Steven: pet club	Anne: cooking club
Josie: film club	Paul: Internet café	

Für jede richtige Einordnung bekommst du 1 Punkt.

LÖSUNG ZU AUFGABE 3

TIPP

Diese Wörter kommen immer nach dem Subjekt und vor dem Verb.
Bei Hilfsverben *(be, can)* kommen sie nach diesen.

Kreuze die richtige Stelle an.

a) I **usually** play the drums …

b) My brother and I **never** walk the dog …

c) I **often** help mum …

d) I **always** go to the cinema …

e) We can **sometimes** play computer games …

f) It's **always / often** fun to make …

Gib dir für jede richtige Lösung 1 Punkt.

LÖSUNG ZU AUFGABE 4

Finde das richtige Verb. Vergiss nicht das Einzahl-*s* in der 3. Person.

Andy **plays** the drums every day. Mr Spencer **lives** in the house next to him. And he **is not / isn't** happy about it. Mr. Spencer **likes** music, but not drums in the evening. He usually **gets up** at 5.30 am and so he **goes** to bed early.

Gib dir für jede richtige Lösung 1 Punkt.

LÖSUNG ZU AUFGABE 5

TIPP

c) *my neighbour's house* wird zu ***his** neighbour's house*

d) *watches* → ***-es*** statt ***-s***

Sag es noch einmal.

a) She often talks about films.

b) She never cooks on Fridays.

c) He plays computer games at his neighbour's house.

d) He watches a lot of films.

e) He makes cakes with the pupils.

f) He likes to walk the dog.

Für jede richtige Frage mit Kurzantwort bekommst du 2 Punkte.

LÖSUNG ZU AUFGABE 6

Setze die fehlenden Buchstaben ein.

a) everywhere b) homework c) interested

d) important e) cinema e) usually

Gib dir für jede richtige Lösung 1 Punkt.

LÖSUNG ZU AUFGABE 7

Du bist Andy. Schau dir die Bilder an und schreibe seinen Text.

[I usually get home at quarter to four.]
First I eat a sandwich.
Then I listen to rock music in my room.
After that I do my homework.
Finally I play the drums.

Gib dir für jeden richtigen Satz 2 Punkte.

LÖSUNG ZU AUFGABE 8

Setze das fehlende Wort ein.

a) living room – sofa / bedroom – **bed**

b) English – England / German – **Germany**

c) bag – exercise book / pencil-case – **pen / pencil / rubber**

d) cupboard – books / wardrobe – **clothes / T-Shirt**

e) write – story / draw – **picture**

Gib dir für jedes richtige Wort 1 Punkt.

MEIN ERGEBNIS

Punkte	56–54	53–52	51–47	46–44	43–39	38–36	35–29	28–26	25–14	13	12–0
Note	1	1,5	2	2,5	3	3,5	4	4,5	5	5,5	6

04

LÖSUNGEN

KA Seite 29

LÖSUNG ZU AUFGABE 1

Hörverstehen 4

Schau dir den Stadtplan an. Schreibe A, B und C in die richtigen Kästchen. Es gibt vier Kästchen. Verwende nur drei.

A:
- Excuse me. How can I get to the information centre?
- The information centre? Let me think … the best way is straight down this road, then turn right at the church. You can see the church from here. Turn left down Yatton Road and the information centre is on your left. It's opposite the police station.

B:
- Excuse me. We can't find the swimming pool.
- Ah, the swimming pool. Well, you can go straight down this road and turn left at the church. There's a bridge over the river. Go over the bridge and you can see the swimming pool on your right.

C:
- I see you've got a street map there. Can I help you?
- Oh, yes, please. How can we get to the museum?
  We can see it on the map, but we can't find it.
- No problem. Just go straight down this road and turn right at the church. Don't go down Yatton Road. Go straight on down Old Church Street. Cross Station Road and the museum is on your right.

Auf dem Stadtplan:
A (Informationszentrum): gegenüber der Polizei
B (Schwimmbad): links an der Brücke
C (Museum): am rechten Ortsrand an der Old Church Street

Gib dir für jede richtige Zuordnung 2 Punkte.

LÖSUNG ZU AUFGABE 2

Leseverstehen

Die Klasse von Mr Watson liest jede Woche einen Text. Dies ist der Text von dieser Woche …

a) **Diese fünf Sätze fehlen im Text. Lies den Text und finde die richtige Stelle (A, B, C, D, E) für die Sätze. Schreibe den Buchstaben an den Satz.**

a) E   b) D   c) B   d) A   e) C

b) **Mach ein Kreuz für ‚richtig' oder ‚falsch' bei jedem Satz.**

a) wrong   b) wrong   c) right   d) wrong   e) right

Für jede richtige Lösung bekommst du 1 Punkt.

LÖSUNG ZU AUFGABE 3

Beantworte diese Fragen zum Text mit ganzen Sätzen oder Kurzantworten.

a) Yes, it has.

b) No, it doesn't.

c) They walk their dogs on the Downs.

d) Yes, there are.

e) Its name is the Great Britain.

f) You can get there by train.

Für jeden Satz kannst du 1,5 Punkte vergeben. Für eine sprachlich richtige Antwort gibt es 1 Punkt, ist sie auch inhaltlich richtig, gibt es ½ Punkt dazu.

LÖSUNG ZU AUFGABE 4

Vergleiche Rachel und Anne.

Rachel and Anne don't play handball.
Rachel and Anne like parks.
Rachel doesn't read books, but Anne reads books.
Rachel doesn't speak German, but Anne speaks German.
Rachel likes rap music, but Anne doesn't like rap music.

Gib dir für jeden richtigen Satz 2 Punkte.

LÖSUNG ZU AUFGABE 5

Schreibe die Fragen zu den Antworten.

a) Do you know much about Exeter?

b) Has Exeter got an old church?

c) Does Liz like old churches?

d) Do you know how to get to Exeter?

e) When does the train to Bristol go?

f) How can you get to the town centre?

TIPP

***Do you** know …*
***Does Liz** know …*
***Does she** know …*

Gib dir für jede richtige Frage 1,5 Punkte.

LÖSUNG ZU AUFGABE 6

Denk an die Stadt, in der du lebst oder an eine benachbarte Stadt und beantworte dann die Fragen.
Verwende nun Fragen und Antworten, um einen kurzen Text über die Stadt zu schreiben.

Beispiellösung:
Erding is a small town in Germany. It hasn't got a zoo, but it has got a park and a swimming pool. There isn't an underground because it's only a small town, but there is a station for trains, and there are buses and taxis. There are a lot of shops and two museums. Tourists sometimes visit Erding, but it isn't very interesting for them.

TIPP
Ob du hier Kurz- oder Langformen verwendest, ist unwesentlich.

Für jede richtige Frage mit Kurzantwort bekommst du 2 Punkte.

LÖSUNG ZU AUFGABE 7

Das deutsche Wort ‚kein' im Englischen. Übersetze die fehlenden Teile.

a) Anne doesn't like cats.

b) Mr Hill can't speak German.

c) This isn't water, it's lemonade.

d) I haven't got my own computer.

e) No idea!

Für die Sätze a) bis d) gibt es 2 Punkte, für e) 1 Punkt.

MEIN ERGEBNIS

Punkte	65–60	59–57	56–51	50–48	47–42	41–39	38–33	32–30	29–16	15	14–0
Note	1	1,5	2	2,5	3	3,5	4	4,5	5	5,5	6

05

LÖSUNGEN

LÖSUNG ZU AUFGABE 1

Hörverstehen 5

Hör der Verkäuferin und der Kundin zu. Die Verkäuferin hat ein Formular. Trage die richtige information ein.

C: Excuse me. I'm looking for a T-shirt. It's a birthday present for my sister. But I can't find the right size.
A: I see. What size does your sister take?
C: She takes medium, but I can only find large or small.
A: Here's a nice T-shirt in medium. What about this?
C: It's nice. How much is it?
A: Umm, let's see … fourteen pounds forty-nine.
C: Oh, I'm sorry, but that's too expensive. I'm looking for something under ten pounds.
A: Oh, right. Look, here's a nice T-shirt in medium, and it isn't too expensive.
C: Oh, well, yes, but it's white. My sister doesn't look good in white. Have you got a yellow T-shirt in medium? Yellow is her favourite colour.
A: I'm sorry, but there isn't one here. Look, can I have your name and phone number? Then I can phone you when the new T-shirts come in next week.
C: Oh, yes, that's a good idea. My name is Sandra Low.
A: Low, L_O_W?
C: Yes, that's right, L_O_W.
A: Thank you. And the phone number?
C: It's 0 one three, four two seven, five one.
A: Right. 0 one three, four two seven, five one. When the new things come in I can phone you.
C: Thanks a lot. Bye!

KA Seite 33

TIPP

C = *customer* (Kundin)
A = *shop assistant* (Verkäufer/in)

Der Text kann bei Bedarf auch zum Leseverständnis genutzt werden.

a) a T-shirt b) Yes, it is. c) medium d) under £ 10
e) yellow f) Low g) 01342751

Gib dir für jede richtige Information 1 Punkt.

LÖSUNG ZU AUFGABE 2

Leseverstehen

Lies den Brief.

a) Tante Helen möchte die Informationen zusammenstellen. Fülle das Formular aus.

a) Sarah b) Saturday c) 18th June d) 3.30 pm
e) 6.30 pm f) the swimming pool in Wellington Road

b) Tante Helen kommt mit Philip zur Party. Sie möchte ein hübsches Geschenk mitbringen. Was würde Sarah gefallen? Es gibt zwei Hinweise in ihrem Brief.

a) a black T-shirt with a picture of the Coconuts

b) the Coconuts' CD "Rock On"

c) Vervollständige den Dialog.

a) 15th June b) my cousin c) at the swimming pool

Für jede richtige Information gibt es 1 Punkt.

LÖSUNG ZU AUFGABE 3

Schreibe das Datum.

a) the twenty-fifth of April – **25th April**

b) the second of May – **2nd May**

c) the eighteenth of March – **18th March**

d) the thirty-first of August – **31st August**

e) the twenty-third of January – **23rd January**

f) the eleventh of September – **11th September**

TIPP

1st – 21st – 31st
2nd – 22nd – 32nd
3rd – 23rd – 33rd
aber: 11th, 12th, 13th, wie alle anderen Ordnungszahlen

Für jede richtige Lösung bekommst du 1 Punkt.

LÖSUNG ZU AUFGABE 4

Frage, was diese Leute gerade tun.

a) Is Aunt Helen looking for a birthday present for Sarah?

b) Are David and Philip making a cake for Sarah's birthday?

c) Is Sarah buying new clothes?

d) Are Sarah's friends singing a song for her?

e) Is Sarah having fun at her birthday party?

f) Are you helping Sarah with the food and drinks?

TIPP

Is: Aunt Helen, she, David, he **is** …

Are: David and Philip, Sarah's friends, they, you, we **are** …

… helping, singing, making

Für jeden richtigen Satz bekommst du 1,5 Punkte.

LÖSUNG ZU AUFGABE 5

Schreibe, was sie gerade nicht tun. Beachte das Beispiel.

a) David isn't working in the kitchen.

b) Sarah and Aunt Helen aren't buying CDs.

TIPP

Aunt Helen, she, David, he **isn't** …

David and Philip, the children, they, you, we **aren't** …

… helping, singing, making

c) Philip isn't writing a letter to Sarah.

d) Philip and David aren't looking for a T-shirt for Sarah.

e) The children aren't listening to CDs.

f) Sarah's mother isn't having fun in the kitchen.

Für jeden richtigen Satz bekommst du 1,5 Punkte.

LÖSUNG ZU AUFGABE 6

Sortiere die Wörter ein.

We haven't got much ...
milk, time, flour, chocolate

We haven't got many ...
cakes, magazines, clothes, packets of crisps, good ideas

TIPP

much:
nicht zählbare Nomen

many:
zählbare Nomen, meist nur in verneinten Sätzen oder Fragen verwendet.

Für jede richtige Einordnung gibt es ½ Punkt.

LÖSUNG ZU AUFGABE 7

Sarahs Freund Oliver / Freundin Olivia hat auch eine Einladung zur Party, aber sie / er kann nicht kommen. Schreibe ihre / seine E-Mail.

Hi, Sarah. I play basketball every Saturday, so I can't come to your party. I'm terribly sorry. Maybe we can meet on Sunday. Then I can give you your present. See you, Olivia / Oliver

Für jeden richtigen Satz bekommst du 2 Punkte. Max. 10 Punkte.

LÖSUNG ZU AUFGABE 8

Setze die richtige Präposition ein. Im Kasten ist ein zusätzliches Wort. Du benötigst es nicht.

David's birthday is **in** July. His party is **on** Saturday 14th July. It starts **at** 4.30 pm. That's when his dad gets home **from** work. His friends can come **to** his house. Then they can go to the swimming pool. It's not very expensive for children **under** fourteen years old. And they can have lots **of** fun!

Für jede richtige Präposition bekommst du 1 Punkt.

MEIN ERGEBNIS

Punkte	63–58	57–55	54–49	48–46	45–40	39–37	36–32	31–29	28–16	15	14–0
Note	1	1,5	2	2,5	3	3,5	4	4,5	5	5,5	6

06

LÖSUNGEN

KA Seite 38

LÖSUNG ZU AUFGABE 1

Hörverstehen 6

Höre Rachel zu. Sie telefoniert gerade mit Anne. Bringe die Aussagen / Fragen von Anne in die richtige Reihenfolge.

Rachel: Hi, Anne. It's Rachel.
Anne: **Oh, hi! Where are you? (1)**
Rachel: I'm on a beach in Weston, near Bristol. But it's boring. What can I do?
Anne: **Maybe you can go shopping. (2)**
Rachel: I haven't got any money. And Mum says I can't go into the town alone. Dad doesn't want to go to the shops with me.
Anne: **Oh, men don't usually like shops. What's your dad doing now? (3)**
Rachel: Just now he's bringing some ice-cream for everybody. He usually sleeps on the beach. My mum usually reads. She doesn't often play with us.
Anne: **What is she doing at the moment? (4)**
Rachel: She's reading a magazine and drinking some water. And my little brother and my sister are no fun.
Anne: **Why? What are they doing? (5)**
Rachel: They're building a sandcastle with a little girl. She's Jack's new friend. It's easy for little kids. I haven't got any friends here.
Anne: **Yes, you have. You've got one friend there. Steven is visiting people in Bristol at the moment. (6)**
Rachel: Steven Hall? Hey, maybe I can meet him somewhere. Have you got his mobile number?
Anne: **Yes, I have. Have you got a pen? It's 0177-239 5714. (7)**
Rachel: Thanks! I can phone him now. Well, after my ice-cream. Bye, Anne. See you soon.

Gib dir für jede richtige Zuordnung 1 Punkt.

LÖSUNG ZU AUFGABE 2

Leseverstehen

Lies den Text über Weston-super-Mare.

a) **Diese Fragen sind die fehlenden Überschriften. Setze sie in den richtigen Kasten. Eine Überschrift ist zusätzlich. Du brauchst sie nicht.**
1. What does the name mean?
2. How can you get to Weston?
3. Where is Weston?
4. What is the beach like?
5. What must tourists know about the beach?
6. What can tourists do in the town?

Gib dir für jede richtige Zuordnung 1 Punkt.

b) **Finde die Zahlen im Text und versehe sie mit dem richtigen Buchstaben. Drei der Zahlen sind nicht im Text.**

A eighty thousand – 80,000
B seventy thousand, seven hundred and eighty-five – nicht im Text
C two thousand and one – 2001
D eighty – nicht im Text
E one thousand four hundred – 1,400
F twenty-eight – 28
G eight thousand – nicht im Text
H seventy-one thousand, seven hundred and fifty-eight – 71,758

Für jede richtige Zuordnung bekommst du 1 Punkt.

LÖSUNG ZU AUFGABE 3

Schreibe, was gewöhnlich oder oft geschieht und was heute oder im Augenblick geschieht.

a) watch – are watching
b) is running – do not usually run
c) builds – is texting
d) writes – is buying
e) reads – isn't reading
f) is phoning – phones

TIPP
*people watch / **don't** watch …*
*Rachel watches / **doesn't** watch …*
*people **are / aren't** watching …*
*Rachel **is / isn't** watching …*
phone – is phoning

Gib dir für jede richtige Form 1 Punkt.

LÖSUNG ZU AUFGABE 4

Setze das richtige Wort in der richtigen Form ein. Hier sind einige Verben, die du verwenden kannst. Du brauchst nicht alle.

The Hills often **go** on holiday to Weston-super-Mare. But this year they **are going** to Torquay. Usually Mr Hill **drives** the car and his wife **reads** some brochures about the place they want to visit. But today Mrs Hill **is driving** and Mr Hill **is looking** at the map. And what **is** Rachel **doing**? Of course, she **is texting** Steven. She never **goes** away without *(ohne)* her mobile phone.

TIPP
to go – he, she, it ***goes***
to do – he, she, it ***does***

Gib dir für jede richtige Form 1 Punkt.

LÖSUNG ZU AUFGABE 5

Setze *some* oder *any* ein.

Mr Hill: Let's go to that shop. I think they've got **some** great souvenirs.
Rachel: Are you sure? I can't see **any** nice things in the window. Just **some** postcards, but there aren't **any** clothes or bags.
Mr. Hill: You're right. But I can see **some** books over there.
Rachel: Books are very expensive. What about magazines?
(to assistant) Have you got **any** magazines?

TIPP
*There are **some** souvenirs.*
*There aren't **any** nice souvenirs.*
*Have you got **any** nice souvenirs?*
***some:** in Aussagesätzen*
***any:** in Fragen und Verneinungen*

Assistant: I'm afraid we haven't got **any**. But we've got **some** interesting books of adventures at sea.
Rachel: But these are very expensive and I can't see **any** cheap books.
Mr Hill: Okay, I can give you **some** money for a book of seaside stories.
Rachel: Thanks Dad! I like to go shopping with you.

Für jede richtige Lösung erhältst du ½ Punkt.

LÖSUNG ZU AUFGABE 6

Rachel schreibt Steven eine SMS. Hier ist ihre Nachricht. Schreibe sie in gutem Englisch.

Hi, Anne says you are in Bristol. Why are you there? What are you doing at the moment? Can we meet on Saturday? I'm on the beach in Weston but I can't see the sea. Hope to see you soon. Be good. Love, Rachel

Gib dir für jeden richtigen Satz 1 Punkt. Max. 10 Punkte.

LÖSUNG ZU AUFGABE 7

Dies ist Stevens Terminkalender für das Wochenende. Es ist jetzt Freitag. Schreibe seine Antwort in gutem Englisch. Beantworte auch die Fragen in Rachels SMS.

Mögliche Antwort:
Hi, Rachel, I'm in Bristol because it's my grandad's 70th birthday on Saturday. At the moment I'm looking for a present for him. We can't meet on Saturday because it's his party then. But I can meet you on Sunday. The 362 bus gets to Bristol at quarter past eleven. Would you like to go to the cinema? Mr Bean is on. See you, Steven.

Gib dir für jeden richtigen Satz 2 Punkte. Max. 12 Punkte.

MEIN ERGEBNIS

Punkte	66–63	62–60	59–53	52–50	49–43	42–40	39–33	32–30	29–16	15	14–0
Note	1	1,5	2	2,5	3	3,5	4	4,5	5	5,5	6

07

LÖSUNGEN

KA Seite 43

LÖSUNG ZU AUFGABE 1

Hörverstehen 7

Einige Schüler der Klasse 8UW unterhalten sich darüber, was sie in den Ferien gemacht haben. Höre ihnen zu und schreibe die Buchstaben A bis E zu den Bildern. Zu einem Bild gehört kein Buchstabe.

TIPP

Hier sind einige Vokabeln, die du vielleicht noch nicht kennst:
mountain sheep – Bergschaf
castle – Burg, Schloss
great – großartig
to stay at home – zu Hause bleiben
sandy beach – Sandstrand
umbrella – Regenschirm

Speaker A (girl): We were in Scotland for two weeks. My parents and my brother and I walked up a mountain and saw some mountain sheep. They ran away when they saw us!

Speaker B (boy): We were in Scotland, too. I thought the old castles were great. We went into one of them and looked round.

Speaker C (boy): We usually go to France, but this year we stayed at home. It was a bit boring, but one day my dad and I took a boat on the River Thames. That was fun!

Speaker D (girl): I went to Cornwall with my aunt and uncle and my two cousins. We went swimming every day. There are some nice sandy beaches in Cornwall.

Speaker E (boy): My mum took my sister and me to the north of England, but the weather wasn't very good. It rained a lot. We bought three umbrellas and went out in the rain almost every day. It wasn't much fun!

Lösung: 1. D, 2. –, 3. C, 4. A, 5. E, 6. B

Gib dir pro richtigen Buchstaben 1 Punkt.

LÖSUNG ZU AUFGABE 2

Hier ist Annes Text über ihre Sommerferien.

a) **Unterstreiche die Gegenwartsformen im Kasten in Grün und die Vergangenheitsformen in Orange. Verwende nicht die fehlenden Sätze aus b). Schaue die Beispiele an.**

Present: is – isn't – speaks – doesn't speak – learn – are – aren't – don't speak
Past: gave – looked at – didn't understand – went – tried – laughed

Gib dir für jede richtige Form ½ Punkt.

b) **Diese Sätze fehlen im Text. Schreibe den richtigen Buchstaben zu jedem Satz.**

D I looked after my little cousins.
E Maybe my aunt and uncle can help me.
A My aunt picked us up and took us to Passau.
C They're in German.
B We went on four different boat trips.

Für jeden richtigen Buchstaben bekommst du 1 Punkt.

LÖSUNG ZU AUFGABE 3

Schreibe, was diese Schüler in ihren Sommerferien gemacht haben.

a) Josh watched movies every day.

b) Steve stayed at home.

c) Christine climbed mountains in Scotland.

d) Martin cooked nice dinners for his friends and family.

e) Janice played lots of computer games.

f) Susan helped her parents in their shop and earned some money.

TIPP

In den Sätzen d) und f) sind Possessivbegleiter zu ergänzen:
my – your – his – her – its – our – their

Gib dir für jede richtige Antwort 1 Punkt.

LÖSUNG ZU AUFGABE 4

Setze die richtige Form des *simple past* von *to be* ein. Zwei Formen sind verneint.

a) The holidays **were** boring.

b) I **was** on a farm with my parents for two weeks.

c) There **were** some nice animals.

d) But there **weren't** any young people there.

e) The village **was** much too quiet.

f) It **wasn't** my favourite place.

TIPP

I, he, she, it ***was***
you, we, they ***were***

Verneinungen mit *to be* ohne *did*:
there ***weren't*** any young people
It ***wasn't*** my …

Gib dir für jede richtige Antwort 1 Punkt.

LÖSUNG ZU AUFGABE 5

Füge die Vergangenheitsform der folgenden Verben in den richtigen Kasten ein.

regelmäßige Formen: played, jumped, wanted, finished, arrived
unregelmäßige Formen: had, wore, wrote, went, got

Pro richtige Einordnung gibt es ½ Punkt.

LÖSUNG ZU AUFGABE 6

In den Sommerferien schrieb Tanya ihrer Großmutter diese Ansichtskarte. Jetzt ist sie wieder zurück in der Schule und die Kinder schreiben gerade über ihre Ferien. Schreibe Tanyas Bericht.

In the summer holidays we went to Padstow. It was nice. There were lots of boats. We went on boat trips but we didn't go swimming, because the water was too cold. I wore my new sunglasses all the time. I took the dog out every evening. He met his new dog-friends and I bought an ice cream at the café. I wanted to meet new friends, too, but it wasn't easy.

Für jedes Verb, das geändert werden muss, gibt es 1 Punkt 10 Punkte insgesamt.
Für jede falsche Änderung, z.B. „my *newed* sunglasses", „wanted to *met*" musst du dir 1 Punkt abziehen.

LÖSUNG ZU AUFGABE 7

Bilde zu den fett gedruckten Wörtern ein Verb im *simple past*.

a) taught b) played c) won d) painted e) found

Gib dir für jedes richtige Verb 1 Punkt.

MEIN ERGEBNIS

Punkte	50–46	45–44	43–40	39–38	37–34	33–32	31–28	27–26	25–20	19–18	17–0
Note	1	1,5	2	2,5	3	3,5	4	4,5	5	5,5	6

08

LÖSUNGEN

KA Seite 48

LÖSUNG ZU AUFGABE 1

Hörverstehen 8

Hör dir den Bericht über einen der Orte auf den Plakaten an.

(Fade in)
… in over a million litres of water. There are sharks, too. You can see fish from all the oceans of the world. It's open from ten o'clock in the morning to six o'clock in the evening, summer and winter. People with a London Pass don't pay anything. For others, tickets cost thirteen pounds twenty-five pence for adults and nine pounds seventy-five for children. You can find us downstairs in County Hall, on the south bank of the Thames. That's in Westminster Bridge Road. The nearest Tube station is Waterloo. For more information, phone this number: o-two-o, seven-nine-six-seven, eight-o, o-o. We close at three o'clock in the afternoon on the twenty-fourth, the twenty-sixth and the thirty-first of December. We don't open on the twenty-fifth of December.

a) **Über welchen Ort spricht der Mann? Kreuze das richtige Plakat an.**
Plakat B — 1 Punkt

b) **Setze die fehlenden Wörter oder Zahlen ein.**
Open every day from 10 am to 6 pm. — 1 Punkt
London Pass: free
Adult: **£13.25** — 1 Punkt
Child: **£9.75** — 1 Punkt
Address: County Hall, Westminster **Bridge** Road — 1 Punkt
Telephone number: **020**, **7967**, 8000 — 1 Punkt
Close at 3 pm on **24th** December, **26th** December and **31st** December. — 3 Punkte
Closed all day on **25th** December. — 1 Punkt

LÖSUNG ZU AUFGABE 2

Leseverstehen

a) **Füge „London Zoo" (LZ) oder „London Wetlands Centre" (LWC) in die Lücken ein.**

a) **LZ** closes earlier than **LWC**.

b) **LWC** is not as expensive as **LZ**.

c) **LZ** is older than **LWC**.

d) **LZ**'s telephone number is easier to remember than **LWC**'s telephone number.

Gib dir für jede richtige Antwort 0,5 Punkte.

b) Einige Kinder der Nelson Schule schrieben über Ausflüge zum Londoner Zoo und dem London Wetlands Centre. Schreibe LZ oder LWC zu jedem Satz.

a) LWC b) LZ c) LZ d) LWC e) LWC f) LZ g) LWC

Gib dir für jede richtige Antwort 1 Punkt.

LÖSUNG ZU AUFGABE 3

Ein Ausflug zum Londoner Zoo. Schreibe, was diese Kinder zu einer bestimmten Zeit gerade machen.

TIPP

*Steve **was** reading / texting / drinking*
*Steve and Craig **were** reading / texting / drinking*

a) At 10.30 Steve was reading brochures at the Education Centre.

b) At 10.30 Craig was texting his girlfriend.

c) At 11.10 Steve and Craig were drinking some lemonade at the Oasis Café.

d) At 11.30 the boys were taking photos of the gorillas.

e) At 12.15 they were eating their sandwiches at the Reptile House.

f) At 12.25 Steve was running out of the Reptile House.

Gib dir für jeden richtigen Satz 1 Punkt.

LÖSUNG ZU AUFGABE 4

TIPP

while → past progressive
when → simple past

Finde einen passenden zweiten Teil für jeden Satz. Füge *when* oder *while* in deine Sätze ein.

a) The gorillas were having breakfast **when lots of people came to see them.**

b) Steve watched a video at the Education Centre **while Craig was talking to his girlfriend.**

c) The boys were sitting in the cafeteria **when a pigeon sat on their table.**

d) Craig was walking through the Aquarium **when a frog** *(Frosch)* **jumped off a wall.**

e) Someone called Steve's name **while he was looking at the postcards.**

f) They were running to the Tube station **when a woman asked them what time it was.**

Gib dir für jeden richtigen Satz 1 Punkt (0,5 Punkte für die richtige Konjunktion; 0,5 Punkte für die richtige Satzzuordnung).

LÖSUNG ZU AUFGABE 5

Vergleiche die Londoner Sehenswürdigkeiten. Du musst dabei alle Adjektive in dem Kasten verwenden.

Beispiele:

a) The British Airways London Eye is more interesting than Buckingham Palace.

b) The Natural History Museum is cheaper than Guinness World of Records.

c) Oxford Street is as famous as Piccadilly Circus.

d) Hyde Park is not as big as Regents Park.
oder: Regents Park is bigger than Hyde Park.

e) The Tube is more boring than the Docklands Light Railway.

f) The London Dungeon is better than Harrods.
oder: Harrods is not as good as the London Dungeon.

TIPP

Hier sind verschiedene Sätze möglich, solange sie einen Sinn ergeben.

cheaper than – not as cheap as – as cheap as
bigger than – not as big as – as big as
better than – not as good as – as good as
more interesting / famous / boring than
not as interesting / famous / boring as
as interesting / famous / boring as

Gib dir für jeden richtigen Satz 1,5 Punkte.

LÖSUNG ZU AUFGABE 6

Du bekommst diese E-Mail von Steven. Schreibe ihm eine besonders nette und höfliche E-Mail zurück und beantworte seine Fragen.

Mögliche Antwort:
Hi, Steven. I'd like to see London with you and Anne. That's a great idea. The best sight for me is the London Dungeon. I really love scary things. I don't want to go on the London Eye because I don't like it when I'm very high in the air. The London Wetlands Centre looked boring on the website, so I don't want to go there. And Covent Garden is just lots of shops. I don't like shopping. So let's go to the Dungeon. I hope that's all right for you and Anne. See you soon.

Gehe bei der Punktevergabe so vor:

Welche ist die beste Sehenswürdigkeit: 2 Punkte

Grund dafür: 2 Punkte

Warum sind die anderen Sehenswürdigkeiten nicht so interessant: 6 Punkte (2 pro Sehenswürdigkeit)

Stil, Kreativität: 2 Punkte

LÖSUNG ZU AUFGABE 7

a) **Bilde Wortpaare.**
burn – fire
fruit – vegetables
palace – royal
passenger – platform

Gib dir für jedes richtige Wortpaar 1 Punkt.

b) Schreibe ein Wort hin, das die gegenteilige Bedeutung hat.

outside ↔ **inside**
best ↔ **worst**
with ↔ **without**
get off ↔ **get on**
begin ↔ **finish / end**
poor ↔ **rich**
full ↔ **empty**

Gib dir für jedes richtige Wort 1 Punkt.

c) Ergänze das fehlende Wort.

a) Mind **the** gap!
b) Stand **clear** of the doors, please.
c) … just the three **of** us.
d) … is bigger **than** St James's Park.
e) … like the back of **my** hand.
f) … how can we **get** back?
g) … isn't as expensive **as** the London Dungeon.
h) … London Zoo is **the** best place in London.

Gib dir für jedes richtige Wort 1 Punkt.

MEIN ERGEBNIS

Punkte	74–68	67–66	65–58	57–56	55–47	46–45	44–37	36–35	34–27	26–25	24–0
Note	1	1,5	2	2,5	3	3,5	4	4,5	5	5,5	6

09

LÖSUNGEN

KA Seite 54

LÖSUNG ZU AUFGABE 1

Leseverstehen

Füge die Überschriften an der richtigen Stelle ein. Eine Überschrift brauchst du nicht.

1. Famous children
2. A normal ten-year-old
3. A very special voice
4. Singing – his first love
5. On the stage
6. How it all began
7. Music in the family

Gib dir für jede richtige Überschrift 1 Punkt.

LÖSUNG ZU AUFGABE 2

Hörverstehen 9

I'm sure you've all heard of Declan. Here's a picture of him. Do you know his song 'An Angel'? It was a big hit here and in Germany, too. My German cousins love it, and it's my favourite song.

Declan was born on the nineteenth of December nineteen ninety-one, so he isn't much older than us. He's recorded lots of songs and he's sung in concerts all over Britain.

Declan's mother is from Ireland. She comes from a large family with fourteen children! And his father is Scottish; but the family now live in the south of England. Declan has got a younger sister, Bernadette.

He started singing at home when he was two years old. When he was seven Declan sang in his first concert, a street concert, and soon after that, he started to perform in competitions. He won one thousand pounds in one year. He saved most of the money but he also bought a basketball, a football and some computer games. He sang 'Amazing Grace' at the Queen's Jubilee when he was eleven, and he also sang at an Elton John concert, where twenty-two thousand people were listening.

Now Declan has started to write his own songs. He's made four records so far, and he's sung on German television. He plays the guitar and the piano.

He's going to make more records, of course, and he would like to be an actor, too. I'm going to watch his website, and when his next record comes out, I'm going to buy it. If you want to know more about Declan, look on the Internet. Here's his website on the board.

a) Unterstreiche die richtige Antwort.

a) a singer b) winter c) two d) toys and games

e) 22,000 f) act

Gib dir für jede richtige Antwort 1 Punkt.

b) Anne entwarf ein Quiz für die Klasse. Hör den Text noch einmal an und füge die Antworten ein.

a) Germany b) Ireland c) eleven d) television

Gib dir für jede richtige Antwort 1 Punkt.

LÖSUNG ZU AUFGABE 3

Vervollständige die Fragen mit der richtigen Form des present perfect.

a) **Have** you **had** …

b) **Have** you ever **used** …

c) **Have** any of your friends ever **stolen** …

d) **Have** many girls **written** …

e) **Have** you ever **heard** …

f) **Has** your sister ever **told** you …

TIPP
***Have** I / you / we / they …*
***Has** she / he / your sister / your friend …*

Gib dir für jede richtige Form 1 Punkt.

LÖSUNG ZU AUFGABE 4

Frage, was diese Leute gemacht oder nicht gemacht haben.

a) Has Wayne bought drinks for the band? – Yes, he has.

b) Has Jo put the lights in the right place? – Yes, she has.

c) Have Jo and Stuart checked the equipment? – No, they haven't.

d) Have the assistants sold the tickets? – Yes, they have.

e) Has the manager talked to the police? – No, he hasn't.

TIPP
Bei bejahten Antworten kommt **keine Kurzform**: *Yes, he has.*
aber: *No, he hasn't.*

Für jeden richtigen Satz bekommst du 2 Punkte.

LÖSUNG ZU AUFGABE 5

Setze das Verb ins *simple past* oder *present perfect*.

Europe´s biggest teen magazine **has just brought out** an article about Declan, and now BRAVO **have invited** him to perform live in their big TV show. Other artists like Sarah Connor, Monrose and Tokio Hotel **have not been** in that show yet. Declan's new single "Love Of My Life" **came out** last Friday and he has **already sold** 100 000 copies in Germany alone. Last year he **sold** about 500 000 CDs in Europe. Declan **has become** very famous in Austria and Switzerland, too. He **has never sung** there on stage, but millions of people **saw** him on German TV in March and April.

Gib dir für jedes richtige Verb 1 Punkt.

LÖSUNG ZU AUFGABE 6

Übersetzung ins Deutsche

|| Aber Declan ist nicht so. || Sein Zimmer in ihrem Haus in Hoo, einer kleinen Stadt in Kent, || sieht aus wie das Zimmer von jedem zehnjährigen Jungen. || An der Wand sind Fußballposter || – er ist Fan von Arsenal und Celtic – und er sammelt Fußballkarten. || Er findet seine neue PlayStation 2 toll; / Er meint, dass seine neue PS2 toll sei; || und seine Lieblingssendung im Fernsehen ist Die Simpsons. || Welche Gerichte mag er am liebsten? Pizza und Spagetti. || Und was wünscht er sich zu Weihnachten? Ein paar neue Computerspiele. || Nein, er benimmt sich / ist wirklich nicht wie ein Star.

Für jede Einheit zwischen den Markierungen || kannst du dir 1 Punkt für Richtigkeit geben.
Die Übersetzung soll als eine mündliche Leistung bewertet werden, d. h. es gibt keinen Punktabzug für Rechtschreibfehler, solange die Bedeutung klar ist.

LÖSUNG ZU AUFGABE 7

Hi, Declan,
I think you're the greatest pop star in Europe! I **have bought all** your CDs **so far**, and **I was at / went to** your last concert in Berlin. **I was || at the front. Did you see** me? **I was wearing** a red T-shirt.
I hope your next concert goes well. I'm going to watch it on TV!

Für jeden richtigen Inhaltspunkt kannst du dir 2 Punkte geben;
Anhaltspunkte für die Bewertung, z. B. Zeitform oder Wortschatz, sind halbfett hervorgehoben.

LÖSUNG ZU AUFGABE 8

Personenbezeichnungen. Beachte die in den Klammern genannte Anzahl der Buchstaben.

a) player b) drummer c) son

d) passenger e) speller f) judge

Gib dir für jede richtige Antwort 1 Punkt.

MEIN ERGEBNIS

Punkte	72–66	65–63	62–57	56–54	53–48	47–45	44–38	37–35	34–29	28–26	25–0
Note	1	1,5	2	2,5	3	3,5	4	4,5	5	5,5	6

10
LÖSUNGEN

KA Seite 60

Für jede richtige Zuordnung gibt es 2 Punkte.

LÖSUNG ZU AUFGABE 1

Leseverstehen

Wähle die beste Sportart, Aktivität oder AG für jede Person.

James	→	**G** Orienteering	Sarah	→	**J** Judo
Pat	→	**D** Fitness	Alison	→	**C** Ice skating
Lea	→	**H** Arts and crafts	Gavin	→	**A** Youth Theatre
Peter	→	**B** Canoeing			

LÖSUNG ZU AUFGABE 2

Hörverstehen 10

Fülle das Formblatt mit Kurzantworten aus.

Eileen Anderson: This is Eileen Anderson. I'm very worried about my son, Sean, that's S_E_A_N.
Doctor's assistant: S_E_A_N. Right. How old is Sean, Mrs Anderson?
Eileen Anderson: He's twelve.
Doctor's assistant: And what's the problem?
Eileen Anderson: Well, the worst thing is that he's got a temperature.
Doctor's assistant: How high is his temperature at the moment, Mrs Anderson?
Eileen Anderson: It's thirty-nine point four. Yesterday it wasn't so high – it's gone up.
Doctor's assistant: And when did this start?
Eileen Anderson: Well, when he came home yesterday he looked hot and he wasn't hungry.
Doctor's assistant: He wasn't hungry? Has he eaten anything?
Eileen Anderson: No, nothing. He usually has some biscuits when he comes home from school, but not yesterday.
Doctor's assistant: I see. Is he drinking enough, Mrs Anderson?
Eileen Anderson: Oh, I think so. He's drinking a lot of mineral water.
Doctor's assistant: And has he got stomach ache?
Eileen Anderson: No, his stomach doesn't hurt, but he's got a bad headache.
Doctor's assistant: A headache. I see. Perhaps he hurt his head at school yesterday?
Eileen Anderson: No, no, he didn't hurt his head. I asked him that. There wasn't an accident.
Doctor's assistant: Right. Has Sean been sick?
Eileen Anderson: Yes, he has. He was sick three times in the night.
Doctor's assistant: Oh, dear. Has he got any pain?
Eileen Anderson: Yes, he says his knees and his shoulders hurt.

Doctor's assistant: Knees and shoulders.
Eileen Anderson: Yes. And his head, of course. He's got this terrible headache.
Doctor's assistant: Right. Well, the doctor can't come to see Sean yet, but he can come this evening at about seven thirty. Give Sean enough to drink. And he mustn't get up, he must stay in bed. All right?
Eileen Anderson: Yes, thanks very much. Seven thirty. Right, bye!
Doctor's assistant: Bye, Mrs Anderson.

a) Sean b) 12 c) temperature d) 39.4° e) yesterday f) no g) yes
h) no i) yes j) three times k) knees, shoulders, head l) 7.30 pm (19.30)

Gib dir für jede richtig gelöste Aufgabe 1 Punkt.

LÖSUNG ZU AUFGABE 3

Stelle Fragen mit *who*, *what* oder *which*.

a) What does Peter love?

b) Who takes him sailing sometimes?

c) What did Lea make for her little brother?

d) Which is more exciting, karate or judo?

e) What can happen to Sarah?

f) Who doesn't want to be fit and healthy?

TIPP

Wenn das **Fragewort** das **Subjekt** ist, dann brauchst du kein *do / does / did*: *Who takes him …*
Ist das Fragewort aber das **Objekt** des Satzes, dann brauchst du *do / does / did*: *What does Peter love?*

Gib dir für jede richtige Frage 2 Punkte.

LÖSUNG ZU AUFGABE 4

Wähle ein passendes Verb und schreibe den Satz noch einmal mit einem Adverb.

a) James finds paths cleverly.
b) Sarah doesn't fight aggressively.
c) Alison skates very fast.
d) Peter swims very well.
e) Pat dances a bit shyly.
f) Lea looks at pictures quietly.

Gib dir für jeden richtigen Satz 2 Punkte.

LÖSUNG ZU AUFGABE 5

Vergleiche Sarah, James und Pat.

a) Pat spells well, but Sarah spells better and James spells best.

b) James reads fast, but Pat reads faster and Sarah reads fastest.

c) Sarah practises hard, but Pat practises harder and James practises hardest.

d) Pat draws beautifully, but James draws more beautifully and Sarah draws most beautifully.

Gib dir für jeden richtigen Satz 2 Punkte.

LÖSUNG ZU AUFGABE 6

Wähle einen Verein aus dem Lesetext und schreibe eine E-Mail an die zuständige Person.

Mögliche Lösung:
Dear Mr Smith,
My name is David Thornton, and I'm twelve years old. My real hobby is football, but I'd like to join the swimming club, too. I can swim, but not very well. I'd like to swim faster. What day of the week is the club? What time does it start and finish? And where is it? Can I get there on the Tube? Please write back soon.

Gehe bei der Punkteverteilung so vor:
You would like to join the club. Say how old you are = 2 Punkte
Say why you want to join = 2 Punkte
Ask about the day of the week = 2 Punkte
Ask what time the activity starts and finishes = 2 Punkte
Ask about the place and public transport = 2 Punkte
Find a good sentence to finish the e-mail = 2 Punkte

Wenn der Inhalt des Satzes eindeutig und für einen *Native Speaker* nachvollziehbar vermittelt wird, können 2 Punkte vergeben werden.

LÖSUNG ZU AUFGABE 7

Wähle das passende Wort für jeden Satz.

a) died b) threw c) sun d) fell e) hurt f) weigh

Gib dir für jeden richtigen Satz 1 Punkt.

LÖSUNG ZU AUFGABE 8

Beschrifte die Körperteile.

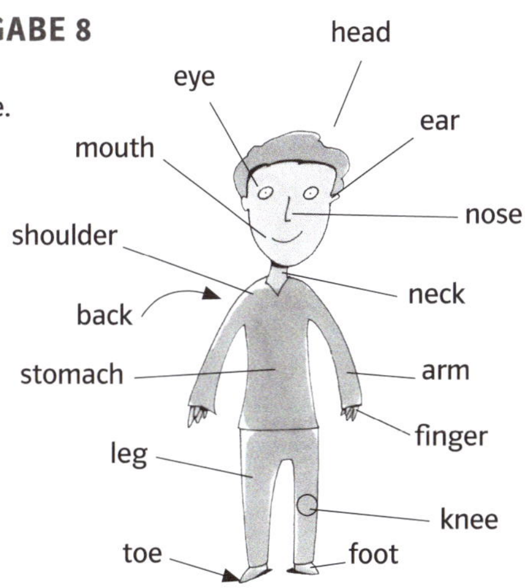

Gib dir für jedes richtig benannte Körperteil 1,25 Punkte.

MEIN ERGEBNIS

Punkte	88–81	80–78	77–70	69–67	66–59	58–56	55–48	47–44	43–36	35–33	32–0
Note	1	1,5	2	2,5	3	3,5	4	4,5	5	5,5	6

11

LÖSUNGEN

LÖSUNG ZU AUFGABE 1

KA Seite 66

Leseverstehen

a) Wähle die geeignetsten Überschriften.

A: A green island **B:** Geography and weather
C: Travel **D:** History **E:** Ponies

Gib dir für jede richtige Überschrift 1 Punkt.

b) Welcher Teil des Textes (A – E) ist am interessantesten für jede Person?

a) D b) C c) C d) E

Gib dir für jede richtige Antwort 1 Punkt.

LÖSUNG ZU AUFGABE 2

Hörverstehen 11

Good morning. It is six thirty in the morning. The breakfast room on Deck Nine at the front of the ship is now open. You can also buy coffee, tea, sandwiches and cake at the cafeteria on Deck Nine at the back of the ship from seven fifteen. We will come into the harbour at Newcastle at nine o'clock. You can get to the car decks from eight fifteen. Please be at your car not later than eight forty-five. When you leave your cabin, make sure you have taken everything with you. Thank you for travelling with Starline Ferries. We hope you have enjoyed the trip, and that you will travel with us again in the future.

a) 6.30 b) Deck Nine / 9 at the front of the ship c) 7.15 am
d) 8.15 e) We mustn't leave anything in the cabin.

Gib dir für jede richtige Antwort 1 Punkt.

LÖSUNG ZU AUFGABE 3

Setze das richtige Possessivpronomen ein.

a) hers b) mine – yours c) Theirs d) ours e) his

TIPP

I	my	mine
you	your	yours
she	her	hers
he	his	his
we	our	ours
you	your	yours
they	their	theirs

Gib dir für jede richtige Antwort 1 Punkt.
Max. 6 Punkte

LÖSUNG ZU AUFGABE 4

Bilde Sätze mit *will* und *won't*.

a) The Irish group *Clannad* **will** give a concert on the Isle of Lewis.

b) But we are sorry to announce that Noel Duggan **won't** be with the band, because he is ill.

Gib dir für jeden richtigen Satz 1,5 Punkte.

c) The Lewis Highland Games **won't** begin on July 14, but one day later, on July 15.

d) Good news for air travellers: Stornoway Airport **will** open again next week.

e) Next month, Stornoway Museum **will** show some Viking equipment. Don't miss it.

f) If you can't come, don't worry. There **will** be some pictures on the website.

Gib dir für jeden richtigen Satz 1,5 Punkte.

LÖSUNG ZU AUFGABE 5

***Will* oder *going to*?**

a) This year Rachel and her family **are going to spend** their holidays on the Shetland islands.

b) Rachel hopes that she **will see** lots of Shetland ponies.

c) And she is sure that she **will be** a perfect guide for her family.

d) On the first day she **is going to take** them to St Ninian's Isle for the Picts' treasure.

e) And she says that she **is going to look for** more treasure on that island.

f) Liz thinks that it **will be** a very boring holiday.

TIPP

going to future: bei Plänen, Vorhaben oder wenn Anzeichen für etwas erkennbar sind

will future: bei Dingen, die man nicht beeinflussen kann, bei Vorhersagen und Vermutungen

Gib dir für jeden richtigen Satz 1 Punkt.

LÖSUNG ZU AUFGABE 6

Schreibe eine Ansichtskarte an einen englischen Freund, Tante oder Onkel.

Beispiellösung:

Lerwick, 23rd June

Dear Fiona,
We're having a great time in Shetland. Yesterday we went to a beach. You can see it on the picture. I like the colours of the boats. We saw a lot of different sea birds there. My mum is interested in birds, so she was happy! Today we looked at some old ruins. That's not my favourite thing, but there were some ponies there, too. I loved them.
Tomorrow we're going to take a ferry to another island. I think there's some treasure there.
I hope you're having a nice time too. See you soon. Love …

Gehe bei der Punkteverteilung so vor:

Einführung: *We're having a great time in … / We're having a boring holiday …:* 2 Punkte

Hinweis auf das Foto: 2 Punkte

Last week / yesterday / today: 4 Punkte

Next week / tomorrow: 4 Punkte

Schlusssatz: 2 Punkte

LÖSUNG ZU AUFGABE 7

Ordne diese vier Wörter in die richtigen Kästen. Schreibe jetzt zwei weitere Wörter in jeden Kasten.

musical instruments	transport	family	weather
bagpipes	helicopter	wife	foggy
guitar	ferry	daughter	sunny
drums	train	father	cloudy

Für *bagpipes*, *helicopter*, *wife*, *foggy*: ½ Punkt;
für weitere Wörter, richtig eingeordnet: 1 Punkt

MEIN ERGEBNIS

Punkte	60–56	55–54	53–48	47–46	45–40	39–38	37–32	31–30	29–24	23–22	21–0
Note	1	1,5	2	2,5	3	3,5	4	4,5	5	5,5	6

12

LÖSUNGEN

KA Seite 71

LÖSUNG ZU AUFGABE 1

Hörverstehen 12

Setze die Zahlen ein, wenn du sie hörst.

A helicopter takes the men to the platform from Aberdeen. The flight takes **three (3)** hours. The helicopter lands on a pad just **fifteen (15)** metres above the waves.
There are **ninety-eight (98)** men on the oil platform, and most of them are over **forty (40)** years old.
The men don't have any days off while they are there. They work for maybe **two (2)** weeks, then they go back to Aberdeen and have **two (2)** weeks' holiday. Everyone works for **twelve (12)** hours a day. They start at **seven (7)** a.m. or they start at **seven (7)** p.m. and work through the night.
There are strict safety rules on the platform. That's because, in the year nineteen **eighty-eight (1988)**, there was a big fire on a platform called Piper Alpha and **one hundred and sixty seven (167)** men died.

Gib dir für jede richtige Zahl 1 Punkt.

LÖSUNG ZU AUFGABE 2

Leseverstehen

Sechs Sätze fehlen in dem Text. Schreibe den richtigen Buchstaben zu jedem der Sätze. Ein Satz ist überflüssig und passt nirgendwo hin.

B Andy puts a body bag on, too. – Everyone becomes rich.
D The helicopter can land.
E There is also a dartboard and a big television.
A They don't look happy. **F** They like chocolate, too.
C When they finally arrive at the platform, the weather is bad.

Gib dir 2 Punkte für jede richtige Zuordnung.

Wenn du dem zusätzlichen Satz einen Buchstaben gegeben hast, musst du dir 2 Punkte abziehen.

LÖSUNG ZU AUFGABE 3

Schreibe den Buchstaben für den zweiten Teil in die Lücke.

a) E b) A c) C d) F e) B f) D

Gib dir für jede richtige Zuordnung 1 Punkt.

LÖSUNG ZU AUFGABE 4

Was wirst du machen, falls du nach Schottland fährst?

a) If I go to Edinburgh, I will look at the castle.

b) If I lose my way in Edinburgh, I will ask somebody.

c) If I hear the bagpipes, I will record the music.

d) If somebody gives me some haggis (sheep's stomach) to eat, I won't eat it.

e) If I see the Loch Ness monster, I will take a photo of it.

f) If it rains (and it probably will), I will buy an umbrella.

Gib dir für jede richtige Antwort 1,5 Punkte.

LÖSUNG ZU AUFGABE 5

***If* oder *when*?**

a) when b) if c) if d) when e) when f) If

TIPP
if: falls: Du bist dir nicht sicher, ob es passiert.
when: wenn, dann: Du bist dir ziemlich sicher, dass es passiert.

Gib dir für jede richtige Antwort 1 Punkt.

LÖSUNG ZU AUFGABE 6

Schreibe über Bobs Tagesablauf. Verwende die Informationen aus dem Lesetext und diese Notizen.

Beispiellösung:
Bob gets up at six o'clock in the morning and has breakfast in the cafeteria. Then he buys some chocolate at the little shop. He's always hungry. At work, the machines are loud. He can only hear the machines. He can't hear his own voice. He has a break for lunch then he goes back to work. At seven o'clock in the evening he and the others finish work. Some more men come to work with the machines. Bob and his friends have a shower and eat their evening meal in the cafeteria. Bob's favourite meal is sausages and chips. He watches television with his friends, or talks about what he has done that day. At the end of the day he's usually very tired, so he goes to bed at half past ten.

Pro Notiz gibt es 1 Punkt = 8 Punkte.
Wenn etwas nicht erwähnt wird, gibt es dafür keinen Punkt.
Wenn etwas sprachlich unverständlich ist, gibt es dafür keinen Punkt.
Es gibt weitere 4 Punkte für Kreativität und zusätzliche Aspekte, wie z. B. *He's always hungry.*

LÖSUNG ZU AUFGABE 7

Finde ein Wort aus A, das sich mit einem Wort aus B reimt.

although – know
daughter – water
ceilidh – daily
fought – short
own – alone
ride – hide
sign – fine
weather – together

Diese Wörter: *now, shout, thing, town* reimen sich mit keinem Wort aus B.

Gib dir für jede richtige Antwort 1 Punkt.

MEIN ERGEBNIS

Punkte	63–57	56–55	54–49	48–47	46–41	40–39	38–33	32–31	30–25	24–23	22–0
Note	1	1,5	2	2,5	3	3,5	4	4,5	5	5,5	6

01

LÖSUNGEN

KA Seite 78

LÖSUNG ZU AUFGABE 1

Hörverstehen 13

It's interesting to watch Simon. Can you see him there? He usually plays cricket. He plays on his village team although he's only fourteen. Just now he's playing volleyball with a few other kids who don't usually play it. He's good with a ball, of course, but he likes to have a bat in his hands. Oh, that was a good shot! He got the ball over the net and right onto the ground. Well done, Simon!

I said that the girls should try football. Look at Elaine. She's playing well. She didn't want to play football, she wanted to play hockey. But she plays ice-hockey in her free time, so I told her she should do something completely different.

Here we are at the cricket nets. They're practising batting. Can you see William? He wanted to do long jump today, but he always does that. It's the one thing he can do. Put a cricket bat into his hands and he has no idea what to do. You see – he missed that ball completely. He's holding the bat wrongly, anyway. William! Left hand at the top of the bat!

Jane is doing long jump. Her real sport is running. She usually wins the hundred metres on sports day. It helps with long jump, too. Look – did you see that? She can go really fast before she jumps … Aah – she hasn't jumped very far – I think she probably started on the wrong foot.

Peter is really good at football, so of course he chooses it when he can. Look at him now. He isn't so good with a badminton racket in his hand, is he? But I think he's enjoying it. Maybe it's because he's playing with three girls. That doesn't often happen on the football field.

Lösung:
Bild A: Peter
Bild B: Elaine
Bild C: Jane
Bild D: Simon

Der Name William wird nicht angekreuzt.

Gib dir 2 Punkte für jede richtige Zuordnung.

LÖSUNG ZU AUFGABE 2

Leseverstehen

Sally: A
Jane: D
Susie: C

Punkteverteilung:
Gib dir für jede richtige Zuordnung 3 Punkte.

LÖSUNG ZU AUFGABE 3

Setze *who, which* oder *whose* ein.

Every year, sports day at Nelson School has plenty of interesting events. At the information desks you can get leaflets **which** give you all the details about where and when the different activities start. In the gym, for example, you can find ten girls **who** present some new dances every hour on the hour. And don't miss the basketball team **whose** trainer comes from America. It is one of the best teams in town. Visitors **who** are interested in the team's trophies can take a look at them in the hall. At 11 am you can see the girl on the football field **whose** goals have become famous. And this is for good photographers: Emily and Jonathan from the school magazine are looking for some people **who** would like to take pictures of the events.

TIPP

who *– people (girls who …)*
which *– things (leaflets which …)*
whose *– things or people (girl … whose …)*

Gib dir für jede richtige Antwort 1 Punkt.

LÖSUNG ZU AUFGABE 4

***Contact clauses* und Relativpronomen**

a) who
b) who
c) –
d) –
e) who
f) –

TIPP

Relativsatz beginnt mit einem Verb/Adverb
→ Relativpronomen: *who usually plays;*

Relativsatz beginnt mit einem Nomen oder Pronomen
→ contact clause: *a girl I have never*

Gib dir für jede richtige Antwort 1 Punkt.

LÖSUNG ZU AUFGABE 5

Präpositionen in Relativsätzen

a) Here's the girl every boy wanted to dance with.
b) Over there you can see the team everybody is talking about.
c) Their captain is the boy a reporter is talking to at the moment.
d) The head teacher now has a ball we wrote our names on.
e) There's the little boy we looked after when he couldn't find his mum.
f) That's the referee those two rugby players ran into.

Gib dir für jeden richtigen Satz 2 Punkte.

LÖSUNG ZU AUFGABE 6

Schreiben

Mögliche Antwort:
27th May
14
tennis
I do it at school once a week on Thursdays in the PE lesson.
I really do it because it's part of my education, and not because I enjoy it. But sometimes it's fun if the weather is nice. I play tennis with my best friend, Emma. We aren't very good at it.

Punkteverteilung:
Birthday: 1 Punkt
Age: 1 Punkt

Where, when, how often: 3 Punkte
Why, how much you enjoy it: 2 Punkte
Who with: 1 Punkt

a) At the language camp I would like to do golf. In golf you hit a ball and try to get it into eighteen little holes. You have to walk a long way from one hole to the next. The winner is the person who doesn't need as many shots than the other players.

What you know about the activity: 3 Punkte

b) My uncle plays golf at the weekends. He says he enjoys it very much because he goes out and gets some exercise. I think it sounds good, so I'd like to try it, too.

Why you would like to do it: 3 Punkte

LÖSUNG ZU AUFGABE 7

Präpositionen

a) Have you got any problems **with** your equipment?

b) John got **to** the finishing line just before Steven.

c) Don't laugh **at** the other team.

d) What happened **to** your glasses?

e) You can't see very well **without** glasses, can you?

f) They are going to show this game **on** TV.

g) Are you interested **in** rugby?

Gib dir für jeden richtigen Satz 1 Punkt.

MEIN ERGEBNIS

Punkte	62–57	56–55	54–49	48–47	46–41	40–39	38–32	31–30	29–24	23–22	21–0
Note	1	1,5	2	2,5	3	3,5	4	4,5	5	5,5	6

02

LÖSUNGEN

KA Seite 84

LÖSUNG ZU AUFGABE 1

Hörverstehen 14

Here we are at the museum. Wait a moment, stay in your seats for now, please, and listen to me. Now, you can leave things on the coach – umbrellas, for example, as it isn't raining, or food, because you aren't allowed to eat your own food in the museum anyway. But just remember that you can't come and get your things from the coach. The driver is going to take it to a car park. So bring everything you need.
You must bring your **money (a) ?** with you. We don't have to pay to get into the museum, although there is a big box that you can put money in if you like. But you might want to buy a souvenir at the museum shop, and you'll need about eight pounds for lunch at the restaurant.
One of my favourites at this museum is a little home on wheels from the nineteenth century. That's on the first floor. You can look into it, but you aren't allowed to go inside. There are also model trains, an art show, some Roman money, some very old things from Egypt, and lots more. You'll be able to pick up a list with a plan in the entrance hall.
Let me see – it's ten fifteen now. You can have just over two hours to look around, then we'll all meet at the museum restaurant at twelve thirty. The restaurant is near the entrance hall, on the right as you go in. And if you need the toilets, they're near the restaurant. You must be at the restaurant at half past twelve. We don't want to have to wait for anybody. Okay, so we'll have lunch in the restaurant and leave at around quarter past one. I've told the coach driver to pick us up at that time. All right? Any questions?

Lösung:
a) C b) C c) A d) B e) A f) B g) C h) B

Gib dir für jede richtige Antwort 1 Punkt.

LÖSUNG ZU AUFGABE 2

Leseverstehen

a) B b) C c) A d) C

Gib dir für jede richtige Antwort 1 Punkt.

LÖSUNG ZU AUFGABE 3

Übersetzung

a) Das weiß ich nicht, aber Sie können Information dazu am Eingang finden.

b) Das sind Räume für Schulklassen, die das Museum besuchen.

c) Das ist im zweiten Stock.

d) Das ist nur für die Sonderausstellung / für die ‚special exhibition'.

e) Gibt es. Eine Kopie von einer der ersten Dampfloks läuft sogar.

f) Ich glaube nicht. Es gibt dort keine Pferde, nur eine Art Maschine.

g) … Aber die Angestellten helfen Ihnen gerne weiter. Sie tragen eine dunkelblaue Uniform.

Gib dir für jeden richtigen Satz 1 Punkt.

LÖSUNG ZU AUFGABE 4

Ergänze die Sätze mit *are / aren't allowed to, are / aren't able to* or *have to / don't have to.*

a) aren't allowed to
b) have to
c) be able to
d) don't have to – have to
e) be allowed to

Gib dir für jede richtige Antwort 1 Punkt.

LÖSUNG ZU AUFGABE 5

Mache Vorschläge und wähle sechs der vorgegebenen Ideen.

Mögliche Lösungen:

a) How about …?
b) We could …
c) I think we should …
d) Why don't we …?
e) Shouldn't we …?
f) Let's …

TIPP

Hier ist mehr als nur eine Lösung richtig. Ergibt der Satz einen Sinn im Englischen, kannst du dir 1 Punkt geben.

Gib dir für jede richtige Antwort 1 Punkt.

LÖSUNG ZU AUFGABE 6

Verwende das *past perfect* oder das *simple past*. Nimm das *past perfect* für das Ereignis, das zuerst stattfand.

a) As soon as the Romans **had invaded** Britain, they **build** forts to protect their soldiers.

b) The Roman general Agricola **planned** a fort after he **had examined** the land at the Rivers Irwell and Medlock. He called the place 'Mamuciam'.

c) After the Romans **had left** the place, invaders **came** from North Germany and Scandinavia.

d) The population of Manchester **grew** very quickly in the 19th century. Until then, it **had been** a small town.

e) By 1850 it **became** very difficult to find a place to live in Manchester because so many immigrants *(Einwanderer)* **had come** to the city to find work.

f) Many children **had died** in damp *(feucht)* houses when Manchester **decided** to build new houses for workers in the second half of the 19th century.

TIPP

Past perfect:
had + *past participle*
had + *planned / grown / come / left*

Gib dir für jeden richtigen Satz 1,5 Punkte.

LÖSUNG ZU AUFGABE 7

Schreiben

Schreibe den Text im *simple past*.

We **had** two hours to look around the museum. We **didn't have to** worry about tickets. We **were able to** leave our coats and bags at the entrance hall. The groups **were doing** different projects, so we **didn't have to** stay in one big group, but we **had to** work in our project groups.
We **weren't allowed to** leave the museum but we **were allowed to** go from one building to another. Somebody in the group **had to** take notes for our project, but we **didn't** all **have to** take notes.
We **were allowed to** take photos, and in some parts of the museum we **were able to** do experiments. But we **weren't allowed to** go inside the old cars, trains and planes, of course.
We **had to** be back at the entrance at twelve thirty.

Gib dir für jede richtig umgewandelte Form 1 Punkt.

LÖSUNG ZU AUFGABE 8

Setze die Verben an die richtige Stelle im *simple past*.

Harriet was alone at home. She was sitting in the living room when there was a knock at the door.
'Who can that be?' she **wondered**.
She went to the door. It was Charlotte.
'Hello, Harriet. Can I talk to you? I don't know what to do on my twenty-first birthday. You're so good at parties and things.'
'Oh, thank you,' she **replied**. 'I hope I can help.'
Harriet thought for a minute.
'You could have a dance,' she **suggested**.
'That sounds like a good idea – but we haven't got a big room at home. Do you know where I can find one?' **asked** Charlotte.
'Well, I think I can arrange something for you,' said Harriet.
'What do you mean?'
'Well, my uncle has got everything you need for a dance, you see,' she **explained**. 'He likes young people, and he's got a big house,'
'Oh, wow!' **shouted** Charlotte. 'That's just wonderful. Thanks, Harriet. I knew you would be able to help. Let's ask him right away.'

Gib dir für jedes richtige Verb 1 Punkt.

MEIN ERGEBNIS

Punkte	60–54	53–52	51–46	45–44	43–38	37–36	35–30	29–28	27–22	21–20	19–0
Note	1	1,5	2	2,5	3	3,5	4	4,5	5	5,5	6

03
LÖSUNGEN

KA Seite 92

LÖSUNG ZU AUFGABE 1

Hörverstehen 15

Steven: Hi, David. It's Steven.
David: Hiya! How's the chicken pox, then? Do you feel terrible?
Steven: No, I don't. In a way, I wish I did feel ill. Mum says I have to do some work for school. What did you do in Maths?
David: Maths? Um, Kevin and I looked at our football cards. He's got more than I have, but I've got some good ones that he hasn't got. You collect them too, don't you? Have you got Zidane?
Steven: Yes, I have actually, but, er, David, my mum's listening to me. I've got to write down the Maths homework.
David: Oh, right, sorry. It's page forty-five, exercises twelve and thirteen. Have you got some paper and a pen there?
Steven: Yes. Page forty-five; exercises twelve and thirteen. Okay, got that.
David: Then there's a problem which isn't in the book, but it's very long, so I won't dictate it to you. I'll bring it round after school tomorrow, okay? I've had chicken pox, so I can't get ill.
Steven: Right, thanks. It'll be good to see you. I'm so bored. Was there any more homework?
David: Yes, English. We have to write about the life of a famous person who is still living. I'm going to look on the Internet for child stars and young people. They've only had short lives so far, so I won't have to write very much.
Steven: Good idea. And is that all?
David: What d'you mean, is that all? It's enough, isn't it?
Steven: Well, it'll keep me busy tomorrow, I guess. Thanks, David! And now about those football cards. Have you …

a) Maths: page **45**; exercises **12** and **13**
English: Write about a **famous** person who is still living.

b) a) B b) C c) B d) A e) C

Gib dir für jede richtige Antwort 1 Punkt.

LÖSUNG ZU AUFGABE 2

Leseverstehen

a) E K L B M J C G H – You don't need: A D F

Gib dir für jede richtige Zuordnung 1,5 Punkte.

b) a) A b) C c) B d) A e) B f) B g) C

Gib dir für jede richtige Antwort 1 Punkt.

LÖSUNG ZU AUFGABE 3

Verwende ein *self*-Pronomen, um das Subjekt hervorzuheben.

a) … he wanted to become a cook himself

b) … Jamie was able to cook a three-course dinner himself.

c) … write the songs themselves?

d) … do all the work themselves.

e) … doesn't have to cook herself.

f) … Jamie himself is talking to you.

TIPP

I	→	*myself*
you	→	*yourself*
he	→	*himself*
she	→	*herself*
we	→	*ourselves*
you	→	*yourselves*
they	→	themselves

LÖSUNG ZU AUFGABE 4

Vervollständige die Sätze und setze ein Komma, falls notwendig.

a) You will quickly put on weight **if you eat a lot of junk food**.

b) If you eat lots of vegetables, **you will feel much fitter**.

c) If you read some of Jamie's recipes, **it will inspire you to cook a meal**.

d) Don't spend your money on hamburgers **if you want a healthy diet**.

e) If you want to improve the lives of farm animals, **don't buy meat from factory farms**.

f) I'm sure it will be good for school children **if they get healthy food at the cafeteria**.

TIPP

Conditional sentences type 1:

if clause:
simple present

main clause:
will, imperative

Gib dir für jeden richtigen Satz 2 Punkte.

LÖSUNG ZU AUFGABE 5

Vervollständige die Sätze mit Konditionalsätzen vom Typ 2. Setze ein Komma, falls notwendig.

a) If people **changed** their eating habits, there **would be** fewer illnesses in industrialized countries.

b) Farm animals **would live** better lives if we **spent** more money on healthy food.

c) If governments in the US and Europe **did not support** factory farms, countries in Africa and South America **would / could sell** more of their produce.

TIPP

Conditional sentences type 2:

if clause:
simple past

main clause:
would, could, might

d) Prices **would be** much lower if supermarkets **did not offer** such a huge variety of products.

e) If school children **ate** healthier food for lunch, they **would concentrate** better in the afternoon.

f) We **would all feel** much healthier if we **did not sit** in front of screens for hours.

Gib dir für jeden richtigen Satz 2 Punkte.

LÖSUNG ZU AUFGABE 6

Schreiben

Lösungsbeispiel:

Dear Jamie,
I read on the Internet that you want to help battery hens. I'm sorry for them and I want to help, too. How can I help? What are you going to do? Have you got any posters about it that I can hang up at my school? It's all right if the posters are in English, because German children understand English very well.
My mum has got three of your recipe books (in German) and she often uses them. I hope you have lots of success with your new project. Please write back soon.

Best wishes,

Punkteverteilung:
Für die Umsetzung der Schreibanweisung gibt es 2 Punkte für jeden deutschen Satz, der in der Liste aufgeführt ist: = insgesamt 10 P.
Für den Inhalt jedes Satzes gilt: genau und in gut verständlichem Englisch: 2 Punkte.
Sind alle Punkte enthalten – aber mit Fehlern, z. B. in der Satzstellung: 1 Punkt Abzug.
Nicht erwähnte Aspekte bzw. unverständlich oder ohne Bezug zur Aufgabe: 0 Punkte
Es gibt 2 zusätzliche Punkte für einen freundlichen Stil und für die Beherrschung relativ komplexer Vokabeln und Grammatik.
Insgesamt: 12 Punkte

LÖSUNG ZU AUFGABE 7

Ordne die Wörter entsprechend ihrer Betonung.

Xx	**xX**	**Xxx**	**xXx**
costume	enjoy	elephant	disabled
difference	advice	paragraph	arrangement
contact	decide	difficult	official
action	yourselves	probably	rehearsal

Gib dir für jede richtige Zuordnung ½ Punkt.

MEIN ERGEBNIS

Punkte	76–69	68–67	66–59	58–57	56–49	48–47	46–38	37–36	35–28	27–26	25–0
Note	1	1,5	2	2,5	3	3,5	4	4,5	5	5,5	6

04

LÖSUNGEN

KA Seite 100

LÖSUNG ZU AUFGABE 1

Leseverstehen

a) Postcards:

a) Karen	b) Rebecca	c) Sarah
d) Tom	e) Tony	f) Sarah

b)

a) Norwich	b) Chester	c) Manchester
d) Llandudno	e) Manchester	f) Cardiff
g) Cardiff	h) Llandudno	i) Norwich

Gib dir für jede richtige Zuordnung 1 Punkt.

LÖSUNG ZU AUFGABE 2

Das Diktat wird zweimal vorgelesen. Das erste Mal in einem normal-langsamen Tempo (Track 16), das zweite Mal nach Sinnabschnitten (Track 17).

Diktat 16

The steam engines in the 19th century needed a lot of coal, and the best places to find it in Britain were the north* of England and South Wales. Soon there were coalmines all over these regions and the cities became the homes of heavy industry. Factories and mines changed the landscape. While the poor lived in tiny houses without toilets, the rich enjoyed a life of leisure outside the towns.

Diktat 17

The steam engines • in the 19th century • needed a lot of coal [comma] • and the best places • to find it in Britain • were the north* of England • and South Wales [full stop] • Soon there were coal mines • all over these regions • and the cities • became the homes • of heavy industry [full stop] • Factories and mines • changed the landscape [full stop] • While the poor • lived in tiny houses • without toilets [comma] • the rich enjoyed • a life of leisure • outside the towns [full stop That's the end of the dictation.] • Pausenzeichen

*Ob hier *north* groß- oder kleingeschrieben wird, ist unwesentlich.

Punkte	Fehlerzahl
14	0 – 3,5
12	4 – 7,5
10	8 – 11,5
8	12 – 15,5
6	16 – 19,5
4	20 – 23,5
2	24 – 27,5
0	> 28

Die Punkte können noch unterteilt werden, so dass z. B. 1 Fehler 14 Punkte, aber 2,5 Fehler 13 Punkte ergeben.
Ein in der Bedeutung noch erkennbares, aber fehlerhaftes Wort = 1 Fehler.
Ein in der Bedeutung nicht mehr erkennbares Wort bzw. ein fehlendes Wort = 1,5 Fehler.

Apostroph- und Groß-/Kleinschreibfehler = ½ Fehler

LÖSUNG ZU AUFGABE 3

Setze ein Adjektiv oder Adverb ein.

a) strange – hard b) regularly c) popular

d) calm – quickly e) difficult – easily

TIPP

Nach *sound, seem, be, become, feel* steht ein Adjektiv, kein Adverb.

LÖSUNG ZU AUFGABE 4

Entscheide, ob du einen Artikel brauchst oder nicht.

a) You can "smell" _ history in lots of British towns but nothing is more exciting than **the** history of Chester.

b) The Romans built **a** theatre and **a** military camp in Chester.

c) In **the** 15th century people built **an** exciting cathedral. But _ Chester Cathedral is not the oldest church in Chester. There had already been a Saxon church there for **a** thousand years.

d) And if you are tired of _ culture, go to _ Chester Zoo.

e) Take a look at its website first. There you can see some great photos of **the** youngest baby animals in the zoo. I like **the** photos of the giraffe best.

TIPP

Es steht kein Artikel bei allgemein gebrauchten abstrakten Nomen:
history,
aber: ***the** history of Chester*

Gib dir für jede richtige Lösung ½ Punkt.

LÖSUNG ZU AUFGABE 5

Was wirst du bis zum Ende deiner Ferien gemacht haben?

a) **I will have taken** lots of photos of animals.

b) **I will have written** fifty pages in my diary.

c) **I will have spent** thirty euros on ice cream.

d) **I will have visited** five castles.

e) **I will have read** two novels.

f) **I will have forgotten** everything about school.

Gib dir für jeden richtigen Satz 1,5 Punkte.

LÖSUNG ZU AUFGABE 6

Schreiben

Lösungsbeispiel:
Hello Tony,
I'm writing to you because you went to Cardiff. Your article was very good. After I had read it, I decided that I would like to visit Cardiff. I sing in a choir, so the male voice choirs will be interesting. I don't live by the sea, so Cardiff will also be good for me because it's on the coast.
Why did you choose Cardiff? Can you tell me about leisure activities in and around the city? When do you think is the best season to visit Cardiff?
I hope that you manage to get to a beach next time you go there. Thanks again for your article. Please write back.
Best wishes.

Punkteverteilung:
Für jede der unten stehenden Aufgaben gibt es 2 Punkte: 1 für relevanten und verständlichen Inhalt und 1 Punkt für Sprachkompetenz.

- Beginne mit einem freundlichen Satz.
- Sag, warum du diesen Ort ausgesucht hast.
- Beschreibe einen Unterschied oder eine Ähnlichkeit mit deinem Heimatort.
- Frage, warum die Person diesen Ort aussuchte.
- Frage, welche Freizeitmöglichkeiten es dort gibt.
- Frage nach der besten Jahreszeit für einen Besuch dort.
- Ende mit einem freundlichen Satz.

LÖSUNG ZU AUFGABE 7

Ergänze die fehlenden Wörter.

a) on

b) makes (für *make* ½ Punkt)

c) his

d) your

e) in

f) of

g) at

h) with

Gib dir für jede richtige Zuordnung 1 Punkt.

MEIN ERGEBNIS

Punkte	76–69	68–67	66–59	58–57	56–49	48–47	46–38	37–36	35–28	27–26	25–0
Note	1	1,5	2	2,5	3	3,5	4	4,5	5	5,5	6

05

LÖSUNGEN

KA Seite 108

LÖSUNG ZU AUFGABE 1

Hörverstehen 18

Hello Debbie, it's me, Sarah. I can't meet you at the playground this evening after all. My uncle's coming from Canada at seven and I have to be there. See you tomorrow. Bye.

Hi, Sandra, it's Bruce here. I don't know if you've already been told, but there's been some kind of problem with a pipe at the sports club. It's just one big lake, water all over the place. Tom's dealing with it, you needn't worry. But there won't be any judo tonight. Can you phone the kids in your group, please, and tell them not to come tonight? I'll be in touch again. Thanks, bye.

Hello Sandra, it's Jenny. I tried to call you at work, but you were in a meeting. Can you call me back, please? It's about the tennis game at the weekend. Thanks. Bye.

Hi, Marcus, it's Gavin. You never have your mobile on! Look, bring your guitar along tonight. Okay? See you later.

Hello Robert. This is Peter Smith. The meeting that was planned for nine tomorrow morning has been changed to eight thirty. Something to do with the plane times of our Japanese visitors, they have to leave early. Anyway, eight thirty tomorrow. See you then.

a)

	Father	Mother	Son	Daughter
Name	Robert	Sandra	Marcus	Debbie

Gib dir für jeden richtigen Namen ½ Punkt.

b)

a) A b) C c) B d) B e) B

LÖSUNG ZU AUFGABE 2

Leseverstehen

a)

	letter	e-mail	text message	note on the table
A				✗
B	✗			
C			✗	
D		✗		
E			✗	
F				✗
G		✗		

Gib dir für jede richtige Antwort 1 Punkt.

b)

A: Marcus ist bei Gavin, wird aber zum Abendessen wieder zu Hause sein. Er hat sein Handy dabei.

B: Debbie hat ein Buch zum Geburtstag bekommen. Sie hat noch nicht angefangen, es zu lesen, meint aber, dass es interessant aussieht. Sie hat die Briefmarke extra für ihren Opa ausgesucht.

C: Der Vater muss spät arbeiten. Er wird erst um 19.30 Uhr wieder da sein und meint, dass die Familie ohne ihn zu Abend essen soll.

D: Sandra bedankt sich für eine Adressenliste und macht darauf aufmerksam, dass es einen Fehler bei ihrer eigenen Adresse gibt – ein „u" fehlt.

E: Marcus will wissen, warum Gavin nicht zu Hause ist. Er wartet bei ihm vor der Tür und niemand ist zu Hause.

F: Die Mutter teilt ihren Kindern mit, dass sie und auch der Vater spät nach Hause kommen werden. Die Kinder sollen sich tiefgekühlte Pizzen machen. Sollte es ein Problem geben, können sie die Mutter auf dem Handy anrufen.

G: Debbie freut sich über Karens Einladung zu einer Party. Sie weiß zwar, wo Karen wohnt, ihre Mutter braucht aber die genaue Adresse. Sie bittet Karen, sie ihr per E-Mail zu schicken.

LÖSUNG ZU AUFGABE 3

Bestimme, ob es sich um einen Aktiv- oder Passivsatz handelt.

a) P b) A c) A d) A e) P f) P g) P h) A

TIPP

Passiv:
form of 'to be' + *past participle*

Gib dir für jede richtige Antwort ½ Punkt.

LÖSUNG ZU AUFGABE 4

Wandle die Aktivsätze ins Passiv um. Verwende den by-agent nur dort, wo die Person wichtig ist.

a) The Internet was invented by Robert E. Kahn.

b) An important book had been written by Leonard Kleinrock some years before.

c) He described how messages could be sent from one computer to another.

d) After that a language for computer communication was developed by Kahn.

e) At first the new technology was used by the US army.

f) Later a lot of money was spent on more research.

g) Today the Internet is used by millions of people every day.

Gib dir für jeden richtigen Satz 2 Punkte.

LÖSUNG ZU AUFGABE 5

Schreibe den Satz neu und verwende ein persönliches Passiv. Verwende hier keinen *by-agent*.

a) Debbie was given a book for her birthday.

b) Sandra has been told about the problem with a pipe.

c) Sandra was shown the problem.

d) Marcus was sent lots of messages.

e) Debbie has not been given the exact address.

f) Debbie was asked for the address.

Gib dir für jeden richtigen Satz 1,5 Punkte.

LÖSUNG ZU AUFGABE 6

Schreiben

Lösungsbeispiel:

Hi Daniela,
How are things?
I'm writing to you because I'm planning to buy a laptop. I've got a computer, but a laptop would be useful on holiday or at my gran's house.
I've seen three interesting advertisements in the paper. The laptop I want is

four years old but it hasn't been used much. It's quite small – 33 cm × 28 cm – so it will even fit into my small rucksack. It's not cheap: nearly € 600. But it cost €1400 when it was new so I'm sure it's good quality. What's your opinion?
You've bought a laptop recently, haven't you?
I hope you can help me because I'm really not sure what I should do.
Write back soon. Bye for now, …

Punkteverteilung:
Für verständlichen Inhalt: 9 Punkte (pro Anweisung 1 Punkt, außer *describe the laptop you want:* 5 Punkte).

Für Sprachqualität, die Wiedergabe der Informationen in dem Werbetext in ganzen Sätzen und Stil: 5 Punkte

LÖSUNG ZU AUFGABE 7

„Falsche Freunde"

a) map
B: It's a town we don't know very well so I'll bring a map with me.

b) sea
A: If you want to get to France from Britain you have to cross the sea.

c) action
B: It's no good just talking. We want to see some action!

d) art
C: Bruce is a computer specialist. Art is just a hobby for him.

e) become
A: It's warm now but it might become cold in the evening, so bring a pullover.

f) meaning
C: What's the meaning of this word?

g) rock
A: There's a large rock in the garden. We have to cut the grass round it.

h) spend
B: I just love shoes. I spend too much on them, really.

Gib dir für jede richtige Antwort 1 Punkt.

MEIN ERGEBNIS

Punkte	70–65	64–63	62–55	54–53	52–45	44–43	42–36	35–34	33–26	25–24	23–0
Note	1	1,5	2	2,5	3	3,5	4	4,5	5	5,5	6

06

LÖSUNGEN

KA Seite 116

LÖSUNG ZU AUFGABE 1

Hörverstehen 19

Kreuze das Bild an, das die Antwort zeigen könnte.

a) Where are you calling from?
b) How many people are hurt?
c) Who's calling, please?
d) When did the accident happen?
e) What have you done so far?

Lösung:
a) 1 b) 2 c) 2 d) 1 e) 3

Gib dir für jede richtige Antwort 1 Punkt.

LÖSUNG ZU AUFGABE 2

Leseverstehen

a)

a) wrong b) right c) wrong d) wrong e) right
f) right g) right h) wrong i) right

b)

a) Heike b) Peter c) Martin d) the coach driver
e) a car driver

Gib dir für jede richtige Antwort 1 Punkt.

LÖSUNG ZU AUFGABE 3

Berichte, was Linda in ihr Tagebuch schrieb.

a) Linda wrote that Heike thought that the English always ate bacon for breakfast.

b) She added that they were having a rehearsal that afternoon, but most of them were too tired to concentrate.

c) Linda wrote that she was going to bed early that night.

d) She wrote that they were going to be shown around Leipzig on the following day.

e) She didn't know whether she liked the city but she wrote that it could be fun anyway.

f) She wrote that Martin was such a nerd because he was only interested in the football stadium.

TIPP

Rückverschiebung der Zeitformen:
thinks → *thought*
eat → *ate*

Anpassung der Pronomen und Begleiter
we → *they*
us → *them*

tonight → *that night* (falls es nicht der gleiche Abend ist)

Gib dir für jeden richtigen Satz 2 Punkte.

LÖSUNG ZU AUFGABE 4

Gib Peters Anweisungen wieder.

a) He told them to go to bed early that day.

b) He asked them to be at the bus at least 15 minutes before they left.

c) He told them not to be surprised about the acoustics because there would be a lot of echo in the church.

d) He told them to concentrate more than usual that time.

e) He reminded them that they were in Germany and that not everyone spoke (speaks) fluent English there.

TIPP

go to bed early
*→ He told them **to go** to bed early*

Gib dir für jeden richtigen Satz 2 Punkte.

LÖSUNG ZU AUFGABE 5

Gib die Fragen von Lindas Eltern wieder.

a) Linda's parents wanted to know where she stayed in Leipzig.

b) They asked her whether she liked the city of Leipzig.

c) They wanted to know what she did in the evenings.

d) They asked her why she hadn't sent them a postcard from Munich.

e) They wondered how long it took from Munich to Freiburg by coach.

f) They wanted to know whether a lot of people in Germany spoke English.

Gib dir für jeden richtigen Satz 2 Punkte.

LÖSUNG ZU AUFGABE 6

Schreibe eine E-Mail.

Lösungsbeispiel:

Hello, I hear you are coming to Munich in July. I'm writing to tell you what you might like to see here. You could go to the Olympia Park because there are some fun things to do there. You take a boat out on the lake, play mini-golf and use the Olympic swimming pool. Another good place is the Alter Peter. That's a tower in the centre of Munich, with a lot of steps up to the top. When you get there there's a great view.
In July the weather will probably be very warm, Bring your swimming things, T-shirts, shorts and so on. But bring some things for wet weather, too, because it does rain sometimes.
It will be great to see you in July.
Best wishes, …

Punkteverteilung:
Anfang: 2 Punkte
Erster Ort mit Begründung: 2 Punkte
Zweiter Ort mit Begründung: 2 Punkte
Wetter: 1 Punkt
Kleidung: 1 Punkt
Abschiedssatz: 2 Punkte
Extrapunkte für lebendigen Stil und einen Sprachgebrauch, der die Möglichkeiten für die 7. Klasse ausschöpft.

LÖSUNG ZU AUFGABE 7

Setze das richtige Wort ein.

a) there

b) to

c) off

d) had

e) put

f) hurried

g) allowed

h) the

i) many

j) to

k) each

l) own

Gib dir für jedes richtige Wort ½ Punkt.

MEIN ERGEBNIS

Punkte	71–65	64–63	62–55	54–53	52–45	44–43	42–36	35–34	33–26	25–24	23–0
Note	1	1,5	2	2,5	3	3,5	4	4,5	5	5,5	6

07

LÖSUNGEN

KA Seite 123

LÖSUNG ZU AUFGABE 1

Hörverstehen 20

A

Anne: No, we want to buy a pass for one of the double-decker buses. I have always dreamed of sitting on top of such a double-decker and enjoying the view.

B

Trevor: Don't worry, we can also sit inside the double-decker, there we will stay dry. The buses have even got heating. But it will be quite hot tomorrow, so we will rather need air-conditioning.

C

Anne: Hm, it isn't very cheap, each pass costs about 70 dollars. But the pass is good for 48 hours and you can see all the major attractions of Manhattan with it. So, in the end, I think it is a fair price.

D

Anne: Well, the good thing about this tour is that we can hop on and off the bus when and where we like. So we will decide ourselves how much time we spend at each sight. Noone will tell us to hurry up and we can concentrate on the really interesting attractions.

E

Trevor: No, you never have to wait for more than half an hour for the next double-decker bus. The buses run from 8 am in the morning until 6 pm in the evening.

F

Anne: I definitely want to see Little Italy, Central Park and the Empire State Building. Chinatown might also be worth a visit. Maybe we can have lunch there!

Lösung:

1. B 2. D 3. F 4. E 5. A 6. C

Gib dir für jede richtige Zuordnung 1,5 Punkte.

LÖSUNG ZU AUFGABE 2

Übersetzung

a) Stimmt, eine Adresse steht hier nicht, aber der Club scheint sehr zentral in der Innenstadt von Manhattan zu liegen.

b) An jedem Samstag tritt ein besonderer Gast auf. Häufig sind das bekannte Fernsehstars.

c) Jeder Besucher muss mindestens zwei Getränke bezahlen. Man hat aber die Wahl zwischen alkoholischen und nicht-alkoholischen Getränken.

d) Eigentlich schon. Die „comedy classes" sind ein Kurs, in dem man lernt, wie man Witze schreibt und auf der Bühne gut präsentiert.

Gib dir für jede inhaltlich richtige Übertragung 2 Punkte.

LÖSUNG ZU AUFGABE 3

Finde die richtige Frage für jede Antwort.

a) a flat
b) an apartment
c) downtown
d) in the city centre
e) underground
f) subway
g) shops
h) stores

Gib dir für jede richtige Antwort 1 Punkt.

LÖSUNG ZU AUFGABE 4

Füge die richtigen Verb-Formen ein.

a) Brooklyn **is** one of New York's five boroughs.
b) You may know that thousands of people **were watching** when Brooklyn Bridge was opened in 1883.
c) Before it **became** a part of New York at the end of the 19th century,
d) Brooklyn **had been** an independent city.
e) Many generations of immigrants from different countries **have settled** in Brooklyn.
f) Presently many artists **are moving** to this part of New York.
g) Therefore some people fear that the rents in Brooklyn **will rise** a lot in the near future.

Gib dir für jedes richtige Verb 1 Punkt.

LÖSUNG ZU AUFGABE 6

Füge die richtigen Formen im *present perfect progressive* und „for" oder „since" ein.

a) Anne **has been looking** for her new school **for** an hour.
b) She is tired because **she has been running for** too long.
c) Her classmates **have been waiting** for her **since** 9 o'clock.
d) Some of them **have been sleeping since** the beginning of the English class.
e) Some **have been playing** Battleships **for** a while.
f) Others **have been doing** grammar exercises **since** the school bell rang.

TIPP

Present perfect progressive:
has / have + *been* + *present participle* (*ing*-Form)
has *been* *going*

for: Zeitraum
since: Zeitpunkt

Punkteverteilung:
Für jede richtige Verbform gibt es 1 Punkt, für jedes richtige "since" oder "for" gibt es 1 weiteren Punkt.

LÖSUNG ZU AUFGABE 6

Benutze entweder *past perfect progressive* oder *simple past* in diesen Sätzen. Benutze das *past perfect progressive* für die Aktivität, welche zuvor passiert war.

TIPP

Past perfect progressive:

had	+	*been*	+	*present participle* (*ing*-Form)
had		*been*		*going*

a) His parents **had been collecting** information for weeks before they **bought** the ticket for their son.

b) They **had been surfing** the internet for hours when they finally **found** a suitable offer.

c) They **chose** a helicopter company that **had been operating** for more than 15 years.

d) Trevor **had been dreaming** about flying in a helicopter since his child hood, but now his wish **came** true.

e) After he **had been waiting** at the heliport for a couple of minutes, the helicopter **arrived**.

f) Trevor **had been flying** for half an hour when he **saw** the Statue of Liberty.

Gib dir für jeden richtigen Satz 2 Punkte.

LÖSUNG ZU AUFGABE 7

Schreiben: Eine sachliche E-Mail

Lösungsbeispiel:

Dear Sir or Madam,
My parents and I would like to go to New York in the summer holidays. Maybe you could help us with our travel arrangements?
We would like to stay there between August 5th and September 1st. Our flight should depart from Frankfurt and should not cost more than $500 per person. Have you got any offers for us? We are also looking for a cheap hotel room.
We would be thankful for information on New York's main tourist attractions. too. Could you recommend any special events that we should attend during our stay?
I hope we are not causing too much trouble. We are looking forward to hearing from you.
Best regards,
xxx

Punkteverteilung:
Für jeden der unten stehenden Aspekte gibt es 2 Punkte: 1 Punkt für relevanten und verständlichen Inhalt und 1 Punkt für Sprachkompetenz.

- Erkläre kurz, warum du die Mail schreibst.
- Gib den gewünschten Zeitraum für eure Reise an.
- Erkundige dich nach einem Flug ab Frankfurt.
- Frage nach preiswerten Hotels.
- Bitte um Informationen zu den wichtigsten Sehenswürdigkeiten.
- Bitte außerdem um Hinweise auf besondere Veranstaltungen.
- Beende die Mail mit einem freundlichen Satz.

MEIN ERGEBNIS

Punkte	70–65	64–60	59–55	54–50	49–45	44–40	39–35	34–30	29–25	24–20	19–0
Note	1	1,5	2	2,5	3	3,5	4	4,5	5	5,5	6

08

LÖSUNGEN

KA Seite 130

LÖSUNG ZU AUFGABE 1

Hörverstehen 21

Los Angeles, San Francisco, San Diego – all these cities can be found in California. There is no American state with a higher population. California offers something for everyone. It is situated on the Pacific Coast of the USA, but also has high mountains, for example in the Sierra Nevada. California's climate is characterized by hot, dry summers and cool, wet winters. Oregon and Arizona are among its neighboring states.
Alaska is the largest state of the USA. It can be found in the northwest of the American continent and is bordered by the Arctic Ocean in the north and Canada in the east. You can find different climate zones in Alaska, but it is generally cold in most regions, with winter temperatures of minus 30 degree Celsius or even less. In summer, temperatures are also mostly below 0 degree Celsius. The biggest city in Alaska is Anchorage, with about 300,000 people living there.
Kansas is located in the midwest of the USA. It borders four other states, among them Oklahoma and Colorado. The biggest part of Kansas in the great central plain is flat. Strong thunderstorms and tornadoes are typical of this state. Moreover Kansas is famous for its grain production. The capital of Kansas is called Topeka, which most Europeans don't know. But maybe you have heard of Kansas City?

Lösung:

a) California	b) Kansas	c) Alaska
d) Alaska	e) Kansas	f) California
g) Alaska	h) California	i) Kansas

Gib dir für jede richtige Antwort 1 Punkt.

LÖSUNG ZU AUFGABE 2

Leseverstehen

1.	a) A, G	b) B	c) C	d) D, E	e) B, F
2.	a) C	b) A	c) C	d) B	e) A

Gib dir für jede richtige Antwort 1 Punkt.

LÖSUNG ZU AUFGABE 3

Adjective oder Adverb? Füge die richtige Form ein.

a) Katja finds her work very **interesting** as she often meets nice people in the restaurant.

b) She is an open person and makes friends **quickly**.

c) It is very important for her to see all of her customers **happy**.

d) Some people are very critical, however, and don't like their coffee as **strong** as it is served.

e) Then they complain **angrily**.

f) Once a customer called her **stupid** because there was a fly in his beer.

g) But even then Katja remained **polite**.

h) However, she is glad that things like that do not happen **regularly**.

TIPP

Nach Verben wie *call, find, imagine, keep, like, make, see* folgt häufig ein direktes Objekt + Adjektiv. Hier wird etwas über die Eigenschaften von Personen/Dingen gesagt.

Gib dir für jede richtige Antwort 1 Punkt.

LÖSUNG ZU AUFGABE 4

Schreibe die Sätze neu in die richtige Reihenfolge.

a) **Very few people know** that blue jeans were invented by a German immigrant.

b) **It has almost been forgotten** that Levi Strauss had come to the USA from Franconia.

c) There are other German people, too, **who played extremely important roles in the USA**.

d) **Albert Einstein completely changed the way we see the world./Albert Einstein changed the way we see the world completely.**

e) **You might be too young** to know Marlene Dietrich, a German actress who became very famous in the USA.

f) **But maybe you know another quite popular German-American actress:** Sandra Bullock.

Gib dir für jede richtige Antwort 1 Punkt.

LÖSUNG ZU AUFGABE 5

Schreibe die Sätze neu in die richtige Reihenfolge.

a) Fernando and his twin sister were born in Mexico in the 1990s./In the 1990s, Fernando and his twin sister were born in Mexico.

b) But their family moved to the USA a few weeks after that./But a few weeks after that, their family moved to the USA.

c) Today Fernando and his sister mainly speak English./Fernando and his sister mainly speak English today.

d) But they often use Spanish at home./But at home, they often use Spanish.

e) They also go to a Spanish club regularly.

f) There they can sometimes see concerts of Mexican bands./Sometimes they can see concerts of Mexican bands there./They can sometimes see concerts of Mexican bands there.

TIPP

Stellung von Adverbien/adverbialen Bestimmungen:
front position
(vor dem Subjekt):
Ort/Zeit/Häufigkeit
mid position
(vor dem Vollverb):
Häufigkeit
end position
(am Satzende):
Art und Weise/Ort/Zeit

Gib dir für jeden richtigen Satz 1,5 Punkte.

LÖSUNG ZU AUFGABE 6

Vervollständige die Sätze.

a) You can come for a cup of tea **at** any time.

b) Whenever he makes a mistake, his wife comments **on** it.

c) Although his grades were good, he dropped out **of** school.

d) **In** my opinion, you should change your hair cut.

e) Look at this house, it is **for** sale. We should think about buying it.

f) Apart **from** apples, I have got everything I need for this cake.

g) I don't like this picture **at** all, it is really ugly.

h) Don't bother **with** the hole in my shirt, I can mend it myself.

Gib dir für jede richtige Präposition 1,5 Punkte.

LÖSUNG ZU AUFGABE 7

Schreiben

Lösungsbeispiel

Many Germans prefer to travel abroad during their summer vacations rather than stay in their own country. The question, however, is whether this is a good idea.

First of all it is important to mention the weather. German summers are sometimes hot and sunny, but there is also the risk of cold and rainy days in July and August, no matter whether you stay in the Alps or by the sea in Northern Germany. People who love the sun might therefore enjoy vacations in a southern country more.

But there are also positive sides to a trip within Germany. If somebody chooses a destination that is quite close to his or her home town, they will usually not spend so much time in traffic jams or in queues at the airport as people going abroad.

Secondly, vacations in Germany are often cheaper than journeys to foreign countries as you generally need less money for gas or train tickets. Food prices are also cheaper in Germany than in some other European countries like Sweden or France.

This is why I think it can be a good idea for Germans to spend their summer vacations in their home country, at least from time to time.

Punkteverteilung:
Für jeden der folgenden Aspekte gibt es 3 Punkte: 1 Punkt für den Inhalt, 1 Punkt für Sprachkompetenz und 1 Punkt für Ausführlichkeit/Anschaulichkeit

1. erstes Argument pro
2. erstes Argument kontra
3. zweites Argument kontra
4. Schluss

MEIN ERGEBNIS

Punkte	68 – 64	63 – 59	58 – 54	53 – 49	48 – 44	43 – 39	38 – 34	33 – 29	28 – 24	23 – 19	18 – 0
Note	1	1,5	2	2,5	3	3,5	4	4,5	5	5,5	6

09

LÖSUNGEN

KA Seite 137

LÖSUNG ZU AUFGABE 1

Hörverstehen 22

The atmosphere here is absolutely fantastic, the audience is just great. Twelve cheerleading squads from different schools have come here to Albert High School today. Presently the girls are warming up, but in about three minutes, the proper event will start.
The cheerleading squads will perform in different categories. Of course they will have to cheer and dance, but they must also jump. Those girls need to be in excellent form today!
We won't see human pyramids today, however. In a human pyramid, some team members have to hold and secure other cheerleaders who are lifted in the air. This is highly dangerous and a lot of accidents have happened because of this stunt.
Each cheerdance routine lasts for about two and a half minutes and is watched closely by five judges. There are a lot of rules for correct cheer-dance routines and the judges have to make sure that these rules are kept by the girls. But they also have to decide which team is best.
Now look at all those colorful uniforms! All girls of a cheerleading squad dress in matching uniforms, and I just can't decide which uniform I like best here. Oh, let me describe the uniform of the Albert High School team: It consists of a red top with three golden stars on it and a red skirt with three golden stripes. Also their pom-pons are golden. In case you don't know, pom-pons are balls made of feathers or strips of paper.
Now the first cheerleading squad is coming into the middle of the gym, the girls are already raising and waving their pom-pons, the competition has started …

1. a) twelve
b) cheer, dance and jump
c) a human pyramid
d) it is very dangerous.
e) perform a cheerdance routine
f) B
g) C

2. a) audience
b) event
c) categories
d) matching
e) waving

Gib dir für jede richtige Antwort 1 Punkt.

LÖSUNG ZU AUFGABE 2

Leseverstehen

a) wrong	b) right	c) right	d) wrong
e) right	f) wrong	g) right	h) wrong

Gib dir für jede richtige Antwort 1 Punkt.

LÖSUNG ZU AUFGABE 3

Übersetzung

a) "Level" steht hier für verschiedene Ebenen im Stadion.

b) Nein, sowohl Senioren als auch Kinder in einem bestimmten Alter müssen nur 50 % des Eintrittspreises zahlen.

c) Hier steht, dass es eine Saisonkarte gibt, Genaueres erfährt man darüber an der Kasse.

d) Ja, anscheinend kann man hier irgendwo für $3,50 pro Stunde parken, da müssen Sie aber auch an der Kasse nachfragen.

Gib dir für jede inhaltlich richtige Übertragung 2 Punkte.

LÖSUNG ZU AUFGABE 4

Kommentiere die Situationen.

a) She should have left home earlier.

b) He must have been very nervous.

c) She needn't have worried about the weather.

d) They could have met much earlier.

e) She might have given him the money for the bike.

f) She can't have forgotten anything.

TIPP

He can't have been there.
→ Er kann nicht da gewesen sein.
He could have been there.
→ Er hätte da sein können.
He might have been there.
→ Er hätte vielleicht da sein können.
He must have been there.
→ Er muss da gewesen sein.
He needn't have been there.
→ Er hätte nicht da sein müssen.
He should have been there.
→ Er hätte da sein müssen / sollen.

Gib dir für jeden richtigen Satz 1,5 Punkte.

LÖSUNG ZU AUFGABE 5

Wandle den unterstrichenen Teil der Sätze um,

a) Many young soccer players hope **to be discovered** one day.

b) They wish **to be praised** for their fast legs.

c) They expect **to be asked** to play for the best football clubs.

d) They wish **to be paid** a lot of money.

e) They can't wait **to be cheered.**

TIPP
Infinitiv Passiv:
be + past participle
be done
Nach Verben wie *expect, hope, want* steht der Infinitiv Passiv mit "to".

Gib dir für jede richtige Antwort 1 Punkt.

LÖSUNG ZU AUFGABE 6

Schreibe die Hausregeln für das *Great Fame Football Stadium* auf.

a) Glasses should not be carried into the stadium.

b) Tickets must not be returned after the beginning of the match.

c) Our staff ought to be treated in a friendly way.

d) All rubbish must be picked up before you leave your seats.

e) The emergency exits should be used in case of fire.

f) Food ought to be bought on our premises.

TIPP
Nach Modalverben steht der Infinitiv Passiv ohne *"to"*.
Ausnahme: *ought to*
Something ought to be done.

Gib dir für jede richtige Lösung 2 Punkte.

LÖSUNG ZU AUFGABE 7

Vokabeltraining

a) B	b) A	c) B	d) A
e) A	f) B	g) B	h) A

Gib dir für jeden richtigen Satz 1 Punkt.

MEIN ERGEBNIS

Punkte	62–58	57–54	53–49	48–45	44–40	39–36	35–31	30–27	26–22	21–18	17–0
Note	1	1,5	2	2,5	3	3,5	4	4,5	5	5,5	6

10

LÖSUNGEN

KA Seite 145

LÖSUNG ZU AUFGABE 1

Leseverstehen

1. a) C b) F c) D d) G e) E f) B g) A

2. a) Last night someone had broken into the saloon …

b) … the sheriff's badge was gone.

c) So he decided to talk to all employees of the museum …

d) He recorded all testimonies.

e) I have nothing to do with this crime.

f) I closed the ticket box a bit later than usual.

g) The last group I showed around left at about seven.

3. David (he already knows about the raised prices)

Gib dir für jede richtige Antwort 1 Punkt.

LÖSUNG ZU AUFGABE 2

Füge das Gerund als Subjekt oder Objekt ein.

a) **Shopping** was Johanna's favorite hobby in Germany and she spent a lot of money in malls.

b) She couldn't imagine **living** in the country.

c) She couldn't stand **taking** walks with her parents.

d) **Going** on an exchange to Texas therefore seemed like a bad idea.

e) But her friend kept **asking** her to come with her to the USA.

f) Finally, Johanna risked **trying** a different lifestyle.

g) On the ranch in Texas she was asked to give a hand, and surprisingly, she didn't mind **helping** at all.

h) **Horse-riding** and horses became her favorite hobbies.

i) **Wearing** a cowboy hat was great fun for her.

j) She loved **making** new experiences every day.

TIPP
Bildung des *Gerund*:
Infinitiv + *-ing*
go + *-ing* → *going*
Funktion des Gerund:
Subjekt: *Reading is fun.*
Objekt: *I like reading.*

Gib dir für jede richtige Antwort 1 Punkt.

LÖSUNG ZU AUFGABE 3

Füge die fehlende Präpositionen und die Gerundien der Verben ein.

a) Many people are interested **in hearing** stories about the Wild West.

b) Some dream **of/about sitting** by a camp fire in the evening.

c) Others are crazy **about travelling** on top of a covered wagon.

d) Most pioneers, however, worried **about surviving**.

e) They were afraid **of not having** enough food.

f) Travelling was especially dangerous if they were bad **at finding** their way.

g) Many of them were looking forward **to settling** down somewhere.

h) Some of them thought **of/about returning** to Europe again.

TIPP

Achtung, hier muss das *Gerund* benutzt werden:
to be used to doing something
to look forward to doing something

Gib dir für jeden richtigen Satz 1,5 Punkte.

LÖSUNG ZU AUFGABE 4

Übersetze die unterstrichenen Satzteile in Englisch.

a) Ben doesn't like the horses eating candy/sweets.

b) He hates tourists treating the horses badly.

c) He worries about John not finding the thief.

d) He is looking forward to his colleague taking part in a rodeo.

e) He is very pleased about so many nice people working in the museum.

f) He doesn't mind John playing the detective.

TIPP

Verb + Objekt + *-ing*-Form
I like my friend telling jokes.
Im Deutschen braucht man einen Nebensatz (dass/wenn):
Ich mag es, dass/wenn mein Freund Witze erzählt.

Gib dir für jeden richtigen Satz 2 Punkte.

LÖSUNG ZU AUFGABE 5

Füge die richtigen Verbformen ein.

a) to set	b) to repair	c) getting	d) hearing
e) to believe	f) chatting	g) to be	h) to find
i) listening	j) to continue		

TIPP

Infinitiv und *Gerund* bedeutungsgleich nach *begin, start, like, love, hate, prefer* (aber nur: would like to, would love to)
Bedeutungsunterschied nach *go on, stop, forget, remember, mean, try*

Gib dir für jede richtige Antwort 1 Punkt.

LÖSUNG ZU AUFGABE 6

Vokabeltraining

A	X	C	B	M	F	N
P	R	O	G	R	A	M
C	E	L	T	O	V	D
Y	T	O	H	B	O	E
F	N	R	E	H	R	G
H	E	I	A	G	I	F
K	C	L	T	I	T	O
P	R	S	E	E	E	T
U	V	A	R	N	N	C

German	American English	British English
Programm	program	programme
Zentrum	center	centre
Farbe	color	colour
Nachbar	neighbor	neighbour
Theater	theater	theatre
Lieblings-	favorite	favourite

Gib dir für jedes richtige Wort ½ Punkt.

LÖSUNG ZU AUFGABE 7

Schreiben

Beispiellösung

John decided to talk to David right away. They had known each other for more than ten years and CJohn just couldn't understand why David would do something like that. When John confronted him with his accusations, David went quite pale. "I, hm … it's not true … why should I …," he stammered. "Come on, David, it's all over now, just tell me why you did it!" John shouted angrily. After a while David began to tell his story. He had accepted a bet to impress his new girl-friend. The plan had been to steal the badge during the opening-hours of the museum and then put it back the next day, without anyone noticing it. But somehow everything had gone wrong. In the end David had to promise John that he would never do anything like that again. And of course, he gave the badge back.

Punkteverteilung:
Je 2 Punkte für die Umsetzung der geforderten Aspekte (1 Punkt für Inhalt, 1 Punkt für Sprache) sowie 2 Extrapunkte für eine lebendige Gestaltung.

Bei eigenem Ende je 2 Punkte für die Beachtung der folgenden Aspekte:
- flüssiger/korrekter Anschluss an das Textende
- glaubhafte Reaktion Davids auf seine Entdeckung
- schlüssiges Motiv
- gelungener Gesamtabschluss der Geschichte

sowie je 2 Extrapunkte für Fantasie und eine lebendige Gestaltung.

MEIN ERGEBNIS

Punkte	83–78	77–72	71–66	65–60	59–54	53–48	47–42	41–36	35–30	29–24	23–0
Note	1	1,5	2	2,5	3	3,5	4	4,5	5	5,5	6

11

LÖSUNGEN

KA Seite 152

LÖSUNG ZU AUFGABE 1

Hörverstehen 24

a) Mr Blank, have you got any other jobs apart from being a juror in a TV show?

b) We all know that the show is like a big party for you, but who's your favorite candidate so far?

c) Many candidates go through hard times just to win. Can you tell us something about the prize for the winner?

d) It is easy to judge other people, but do you play any instruments yourself?

e) I have heard that we won't see you on TV next year. So what are your plans?

a) B b) A c) C d) B e) C

Gib dir für jede richtige Antwort ½ Punkt.

LÖSUNG ZU AUFGABE 2

Leseverstehen

a) Adrian	b) Brian	c) Toby	d) Vicky
e) Lily	f) Lily	g) Vicky	h) Adrian
i) Brian	j) Toby		

Gib dir für jede richtige Zuordnung 1 Punkt.

LÖSUNG ZU AUFGABE 3

Übersetzung

a) You have to be between 16 and 30 years old. And you have to be able to move well on a stage.

b) The winners of the casting can take part in a TV show called "Germany sings".

c) No, you can also phone Mrs Krach or send a mail to her.

d) They want to know whether you can play an instrument and how long you have been playing it for. Then they ask if you have any further talents like dancing or acting. And of course you have to tell them the name of the song you want to perform during the casting.

Punkteverteilung:
a) 4 Punkte
(pro Aspekt 2 Punkte)
b) 2 Punkte
c) 2 Punkte
d) 6 Punkte
(pro Aspekt 2 Punkte)

LÖSUNG ZU AUFGABE 4

Füge die richtigen Passivformen der Verben ein.

a) British rock and pop bands can **be heard** on the radio every day.

b) One of the first bands that **was loved** by German fans were the Beatles.

c) The band **was formed** in Liverpool in 1960, but the Beatles also spent a lot of time in Hamburg in their early years.

d) Their records **have been bought** by millions of fans up to today.

e) After the charts **had been dominated** by their songs for many years, the Beatles split up in 1970.

f) Even today many tears **are cried** because this band doesn't exist anymore.

g) Some fans think that the Beatles' success **will never be repeated** by another band.

TIPP

Passiv:
Form von "to be" + *past participle (+ by-agent)*
simple present:
it is seen
(by many people)
simple past:
it was seen
present perfect:
it has been seen
past perfect:
it had been seen
will-future:
it will be seen
infinitive:
(to) be seen

Gib dir für jeden richtigen Satz 1 Punkt.

LÖSUNG ZU AUFGABE 5

Füge das Verb im *present progressive* oder *past progressive passive* ein.

a) Many fashion items that **are being worn** at the moment have a strange history.

b) Currently, baggy pants **are being considered** a basic piece of clothing by many boys, especially those who like Rap or HipHop.

c) Many say that baggy pants **were being invented** by gangsters while they were in prison.

d) The typical prison outfit without a belt **was being turned** into a fashion statement.

e) Later baggy pants **were being used** by Rappers as a sign of toughness when there were gang fights.

f) Nowadays these pants **are still being seen** as a sign of a bad character by some people.

g) Laws against baggy pants **are being discussed** in some American states at the moment.

TIPP

Verlaufsformen des Passivs:
Form von to be + being + *past participle (+ by-agent)*
present progressive:
it is being discussed
(by many people)
past progressive:
it was being discussed

Gib dir für jeden richtigen Satz 1 Punkt.

LÖSUNG ZU AUFGABE 6

TIPP

Verb + Präposition im Aktivsatz:
He looks after the cat well.
Im Passivsatz steht die Präposition ebenfalls gleich nach dem Verb:
The cat *is looked after* well.

Wandle die Sätze ins Passiv um.

a) Punk rock has been written about by music journalists for years.

b) The dangers of the punk movement were worried about by parents in the early eighties.

c) Many punks had already been dealt with by the police.

d) Empty houses were broken into by some punks to live there.

e) High politicians were made fun of by punk bands like the *Sex Pistols*.

f) The early days of the punk movement are still talked about by young punks today.

Gib dir für jeden richtigen Satz 2 Punkte.

LÖSUNG ZU AUFGABE 7

Wortschatz

a) She couldn't **believe** her eyes.

b) I don't know how to **put** it into words.

c) They **fell** in love with each other at once.

d) **Get** out of my sight, Mike!

e) They **took** turns cooking the meals.

f) I'd really like to **take** part in it.

Gib dir für jedes richtige Verb 1 Punkt.

MEIN ERGEBNIS

Punkte	61–58	57–53	52–49	48–44	43–40	39–35	34–31	30–26	25–22	21–17	16–0
Note	1	1,5	2	2,5	3	3,5	4	4,5	5	5,5	6

12 LÖSUNGEN

KA Seite 160

LÖSUNG ZU AUFGABE 1

Leseverstehen

a) B b) A c) C d) C e) B f) A

Gib dir für jede richtige Zuordnung 1,5 Punkte.

LÖSUNG ZU AUFGABE 2

Unterstreiche die Ausdrücke, die Jack nicht in diesem formalen Telefongespräch benutzen sollte.

a) <u>Hey dude</u>, I'm <u>kinda</u> interested in the job at your pizza restaurant.

b) Sarah, a <u>buddy</u> of mine, is already working at your place, and she's like, you need more people in the kitchen.

c) I <u>dunno</u> a lot about cooking, but I have done a <u>lotta</u> different jobs.

d) Well, people <u>go</u>, I'm a quick learner <u>big time</u>, so this shouldn't be a problem.

e) Yes, can you <u>gimme</u> some information on the <u>bucks</u> I would get?

Gib dir für jedes richtige Wort 1 Punkt.

LÖSUNG ZU AUFGABE 3

Schreibe vollständige Sätze.

a) Mr Fry wants the pizza-baker to work fast.

b) He expects his restaurant to be busy.

c) He prefers his staff to use fresh food.

d) He advises the waiters to learn some Italian.

e) He tells everyone to be patient with the guests.

f) He asks his guests to try the delicious pizza.

TIPP
Ich möchte/will, <u>dass</u> jemand etwas tut.
I want/would like somebody <u>to</u> do something.

Gib dir für jeden richtigen Satz 2 Punkte.

LÖSUNG ZU AUFGABE 4

Schreibe Bobs Fragen um.

a) Bob wonders whether to take an umbrella with him.

b) He wants to know what to do if he gets lost.

c) He is not sure where to sit down to take a break.

TIPP
Englisch: Infinitiv nach Fragewort:
He wonders <u>what to do</u>.
Deutsch: Nebensatz mit Modalverb:
Er fragt sich <u>was er tun soll</u>.

d) He has no idea what to do if he is late.

e) He doesn't remember whether to work every Saturday.

f) He wants to be told when to start his new job.

Gib dir für jeden richtigen Satz 1,5 Punkte.

LÖSUNG ZU AUFGABE 5

Vervollständige, was sie sagt, mit den Informationen aus dem Kasten.

a) He was the first to do a bungee-jump.

b) She was the only one to make lunch.

c) He was the last to reach the top of the mountain.

d) She was the youngest girl to go to the camp.

e) She was the best partner to sing with.

f) He was the most interesting boy to listen to.

TIPP
Englisch: Infinitiv nach "the first", "the last", "the only one", Superlativen:
He is the first to go.
Deutsch: Relativsatz:
Er war der Erste, der ging.

Gib dir für jeden richtigen Satz 1,5 Punkte.

LÖSUNG ZU AUFGABE 6

Kombiniere zwei Sätze und forme einen Satz daraus.

a) Many teenagers, for whom communication is very important, own cell phones.

b) The term "texting", which is called "simsen" in German, refers to the exchange of short written messages.

c) Extravagant ring tones for cell phones, which are often parts of well-known songs, are very popular.

d) The first cell phone, whose modern version can be put into a pants pocket, was almost as big as a brick.

e) There are many family arguments because of cell phones, whose costs are often high.

TIPP
Notwendiger Relativsatz *(defining relative clause)*:
- Hauptsatz ist ohne Relativsatz unvollständig/unverständlich
- kein Komma zwischen Hauptsatz und Relativsatz
- Relativpronomen: who/that, whom, which/that, whose

Nicht notwendiger Relativsatz *(non-defining relative clause)*:
- Zusatzinfos zum Hauptsatz
- Komma zwischen Hauptsatz und Relativsatz
- Relativpronomen: who, whom, which, whose

Gib dir für jeden richtigen Satz 2 Punkte.

LÖSUNG ZU AUFGABE 7

Schreiben

Lösungsbeispiel

Dear Mrs Sunny,

Thank you very much for your letter. I can understand that you are really in trouble and will try to help you and give you some advice.
First of all you should talk to your son and find out why he finds computer games so fascinating. Perhaps you can think of other activities that you two could do together and that he might find equally exciting.
Secondly, try to think of a compromise with your son. Maybe he can play games for half an hour every day after he has done his homework?
Thirdly, he should only be allowed to keep the computer in his room if he sticks to your rules. If not, you should put the computer into the living-room or another room where you can control what he is doing with it.
I hope that you will be able to solve the problems with your son and find a way that is acceptable for both of you.

Yours
Cathy Wise

Punkteverteilung:
Anfang: 2 Punkte
Erster Vorschlag zur Verbesserung der Situation: 2 Punkte
Zweiter Vorschlag zur Verbesserung der Situation: 2 Punkte
Dritter Vorschlag zur Verbesserung der Situation: 2 Punkte
Ende/Abschied: 2 Punkte
2 Extrapunkte für lebendigen Stil und einen Sprachgebrauch, der die Möglichkeiten der 8. Klasse ausschöpft

MEIN ERGEBNIS

Punkte	71–66	65–61	60–56	55–51	50–46	45–41	40–36	35–31	30–26	25–21	20–0
Note	1	1,5	2	2,5	3	3,5	4	4,5	5	5,5	6

Topfit in die nächste Klassenarbeit!

Klassenarbeiten wie in der Schule

- 24 Klassenarbeiten zu allen wichtigen Themen der Klassen 5 – 8 zeigen dir, was drankommen kann.
- Die Zeitvorgabe und die vorgegebenen Punkte für jede Aufgabe schaffen eine „echte" Klassenarbeitssituation
- Lösungen mit Tipps und genaue Hinweise zur Punktevergabe ermöglichen dir das selbstständige Korrigieren
- Hast du die Punkte zusammengezählt, kannst du direkt deine Note ablesen und weißt genau, wie gut du bist!

Klassenarbeiten wie in der Schule
Deutsch 5. – 8. Klasse
Gymnasium
ISBN 978-3-12-927212-1

Klassenarbeiten wie in der Schule
Mathematik 5. – 8. Klasse
Gymnasium
ISBN 978-3-12-927214-5

Diese und weitere Klett-Lernhilfen sind im Buchhandel erhältlich.
Weitere Informationen unter **www.klett.de/lernhilfen**